Transformative Arts

Transformative Arts

Biological, Digital, and Everyday Aesthetics

Gary A. Berg

ROWMAN & LITTLEFIELD
Lanham • Boulder • New York • London

Published by Rowman & Littlefield
An imprint of The Rowman & Littlefield Publishing Group, Inc.
4501 Forbes Boulevard, Suite 200, Lanham, Maryland 20706
www.rowman.com

86-90 Paul Street, London EC2A 4NE, United Kingdom

Copyright © 2024 by Gary A. Berg

All rights reserved. No part of this book may be reproduced in any form or by any electronic or mechanical means, including information storage and retrieval systems, without written permission from the publisher, except by a reviewer who may quote passages in a review.

British Library Cataloguing in Publication Information Available

Library of Congress Cataloging-in-Publication Data

Names: Berg, Gary A., 1955– author.
Title: Transformative arts : biological, digital, and everyday aesthetics / Gary A. Berg.
Description: Lanham : Rowman & Littlefield, [2024] | Includes bibliographical references. | Summary: "Drawing on an extensive yet concise review of the history of cross-cultural aesthetics, the volume presents the scientists and artists working in the new world of transformative arts"—Provided by publisher.
Identifiers: LCCN 2023046909 (print) | LCCN 2023046910 (ebook) | ISBN 9781475872521 (cloth) | ISBN 9781475872538 (paperback) | ISBN 9781475872545 (epub)
Subjects: LCSH: Aesthetics—Cross-cultural studies. | Art and technology. | Art and biology. | Personality and creative ability.
Classification: LCC BH301.C92 B47 2024 (print) | LCC BH301.C92 (ebook) | DDC 701/.17—dc23/eng/20231120
LC record available at https://lccn.loc.gov/2023046909
LC ebook record available at https://lccn.loc.gov/2023046910

Contents

List of Tables and Figures	ix
Acknowledgments	xi
Introduction	1
Starting Point	5
Shaping Questions	6
Plan for the Book	8
Conclusion	11
Chapter 1: The Origin and Evolution of Western Aesthetics	15
Philosophical Foundations	15
Spirituality and Art	18
Religious Traditions and Art	18
The Sublime and Transcendence	21
Modern and Contemporary Scholars on Art and Spirituality	23
Modern Aesthetics	25
Psychological Perspectives	28
Conclusion	31
Chapter 2: Beyond Western Aesthetics	37
Anthropological Foundations	37
Regional Histories and Contrasts	41
Cross-cultural Patterns	47

Beauty in Disinterestedness	47
Beauty of Spirituality and Transcendence	49
Beauty of Imperfection and Process	53
Beauty Every Day	55
Conclusion	60
Chapter 3: The Aesthetics of the Everyday	65
European Precursors	65
John Dewey and *Art as Experience*	67
Aesthetics of the Everyday	70
Conclusion	75
Chapter 4: Digital Art	79
Origins	81
Machine Learning and Art	86
Deep Learning	88
Generative Adversarial Networks	89
Applications Using Text Prompts to Create Art	90
Robotics	92
Computers in Music and Literature	98
Computers and Performing Arts	100
Computers and Consciousness	104
Conclusion	105
Chapter 5: Biological Art	113
Using Technology to Uncover Beauty Up Close and Far Away	116
Animal Art	119
Development of Bio Art	123

Humans Interacting with Living Organisms	125
Conclusion	130
Conclusion	135
Primary Questions	135
Impact of Computer and Biological Advancements on Aesthetics	136
Power of Everyday Aesthetics	138
Conclusion	141
Bibliography	143

List of Tables and Figures

TABLES

5.1.	Organisms in Bio Art	116
c.1.	Traditional Versus New Aesthetics	137

FIGURES

i.1.	Mycoplasma pneumoniae, bacteria	3
i.2.	Tissue Culture & Art Project	4
i.3.	Artsbot Robots at Work	4
i.4.	*The Frozen Wild Dnieper River*	11
2.1.	Celt with Incised Profile	39
2.2.	*Reciting Poetry Before the Yellowing of Autumn*	43
2.3.	Banshō Zukan	44
2.4.	Designs from the Adina Mosque, Pandua, West Bengal	45
2.5.	Japanese Landscape	48
2.6.	*Shiva as the Lord of Dance*	52
2.7.	*Evening Rain at Karasaki*	54
2.8.	*Tea Ceremony Apparatus*	56
2.9.	Cold-water Container for Tea	57
2.10.	Eskimo Carving	59

4.1.	*Gaussian-Quadratic*	83
4.2.	*Photo-elastic Walk*	85
4.3.	Traditional Programming Versus Machine Learning	87
4.4.	DALLE-2 Generated Image	91
4.5.	A Postulated Interior of the Duck of Vaucanson (1738–1739)	93
4.6.	Alfred Jarry, Marionnette from Original Production of *Ubu Roi*	94
4.7.	Robocygne	95
4.8.	Reclining StickMan—2020 Adelaide Biennial of Australian Art	96
4.9.	Artsbot Painting	97
4.10.	FAR, Company Wayne McGregor, 2010	102
4.11.	*Danceroom Spectroscopy*	103
4.12.	Unsupervised—Machine Hallucinations—MoMA	106
5.1.	Bio Art Terminology	114
5.2.	Fibrous Configuration of a Dry Macrofoam Sponge Swab	117
5.3.	A View of Earth from Saturn	118
5.4.	Lolo and the Pranksters 1910	121
5.5.	Installation View of the Exhibition, *Edward Steichen's Delphiniums*	123
5.6.	Algae Digital Kaleidoscope & Tapestry	125
5.7.	*Attracted to Light*	126
5.8.	*Coherence*	127
5.9.	Star Diagram	127
5.10.	*The Honeycomb Vase "Made by Bees"*	129
5.11.	Tissue Culture & Art Project	130
c.1.	Galaxy Cluster SMACS 0723	136

Acknowledgments

The collections and online resources of the libraries of the City of Los Angeles and UCLA, especially the Arts Library, were used extensively in the research done for this book. The use of images in this book from the government, library, and individual artists and scientists is greatly appreciated. The institutions include CDC, LACMA, the Library of Congress, the Metropolitan Museum of Art, MIT, NASA, and the Smithsonian Libraries. A special thanks to the cooperating artists and scientists Refik Anadol, Lars Asplund, Oron Catts, David R. Glowacki, Sarah Grant, Alexander Larsson, Mick Lorusso, Wayne McGregor, Geoffrey Mann, Leonel Moura, Michael A. Noll, Jennifer Parker, Stelarc, Åsa and Carl Unander-Scharin, and Ionat Zurr.

I want to thank those who read parts or all the manuscript in progress, including Alec Berg for the digital arts chapter. Once again, I am indebted to Dr. Linda Venis for carefully reviewing the manuscript and thoughtful discussion throughout the writing process.

Introduction

What is art, and who is an artist? These simple questions have challenged philosophers throughout human history, but the essential theoretical knot is unraveling. Staggering advances in computer science and biotechnology contest the distinctions among human, machine, and biologically created art forms. Artificial intelligence and genetic manipulation are no longer just tools but avenues for artists to collaborate in creating new art forms and content.

While there is dispute about whether there can be non-human artists, at the very least we are discovering through machine learning and biotechnology that creativity is pervasive. What's more, scientists are uncovering principles that lead to better understanding human-centered creativity and aesthetics.

At the same time, the lamented death of art following the rise of modern art theory and the reframing brought about by the appreciation of non-Western cultures leads to the budding philosophy of everyday aesthetics. John Dewey and his influential book *Art as Experience* was a precursor to the emerging field, positing the possibility of artistic encounters of non-art objects and events. Emerging from American philosophical traditions and cross-cultural art forms, this thinking reveals awareness of the way art permeates daily life.

Traditional fine arts are often regarded as rarefied, something accessed by the uniquely talented and displayed in impressive museums or on lavish stages in front of large audiences. Art thusly conceived is something that most people never practice in their lives. Yet in day-to-day life, we all experience a creative satisfaction through interaction with the physical and social environment, which is a form of artistic practice. The everyday aesthetics contemporary movement within the field of philosophy of art rejects distinctions such as those between fine and popular art, or art and craft.

A central aspect of considering the aesthetics of the familiar necessitates turning to non-Western traditions. Creating and appreciating beauty is often a social experience leading to a greater capacity to understand others and adapt to their way of thinking and live in an increasingly multicultural world. In contrast to Western traditions, Eastern aesthetics suggests that ordered structure contrives, logical exposition falsifies, and linear, consecutive argument eventually limits.

Humans elaborate daily life beyond what is practical and directly functional. Some argue that a key evolutionary advantage of humans is the drive to evolve and progress as a social group through such seemingly non-essential inventiveness. Making art may link to a deep biological, primaeval purpose and delight in humans, and perhaps in plants and animals as well.

Taking a cultural evolutionary perspective, Mihaly Csikszentmihalyi, the psychologist researching creativity and artists, argues that invention in the arts, religion, political systems, the sciences, and technologies are stages along the path of cultural evolution: "To be human means to be creative." In this way, the evolution of human culture is important for our continued existence: "If the right memes are selected, we survive; otherwise we do not."[1]

Some suggest that art is a fundamental characteristic of all living things, and that we need to move away from a human-centered conception of aesthetics. In this way, the development of biotechnology marks the rise of a new medium for artists, as well as an enlarged conception of what we consider art. Rapid advances lead to new art forms involving both a simple appreciation of nature previously unseen on the molecular level, and tools with which artists can manipulate and collaborate creatively with nature.

The highly diverse field of biological or bio art includes works that appreciate the beauty of nature in creating images of rarely seen features of nature, as well as direct manipulations of nature for specific purposes. One fascinating example of bio art is the Tissue Culture & Art Project, which explores the manipulation of living tissues as a medium for artistic expression. The leaders, Oron Catts and Ionat Zurr, create "semi-living" entities grown in artificial conditions that imitate body conditions—in semi-living sculptures. The goal of this work is to culture and sustain tissue constructs of varying complexity, and by that creative process, to challenge and focus attention on perceptions about the utilization of new biological knowledge.[2]

Can this same pattern of evolutionary creativity exist outside the biological world? Blaise Agüera y Arcas, a leader of Google's AI group and founder of the Artists and Machine Intelligence program, claims that the transformation of artistic practice and theory began with the 19th-century photography revolution, and is a parallel to the current revolution of art through machine intelligence. He sees the revolution as promising to democratize the means of reproduction and production of art.[3]

Although creating art using artificial intelligence (AI) techniques is relatively new, artists have used algorithms, automation, and computation to create art for decades. Applications are now effectively employing AI to create images and text, based on simple prompts requiring no computer

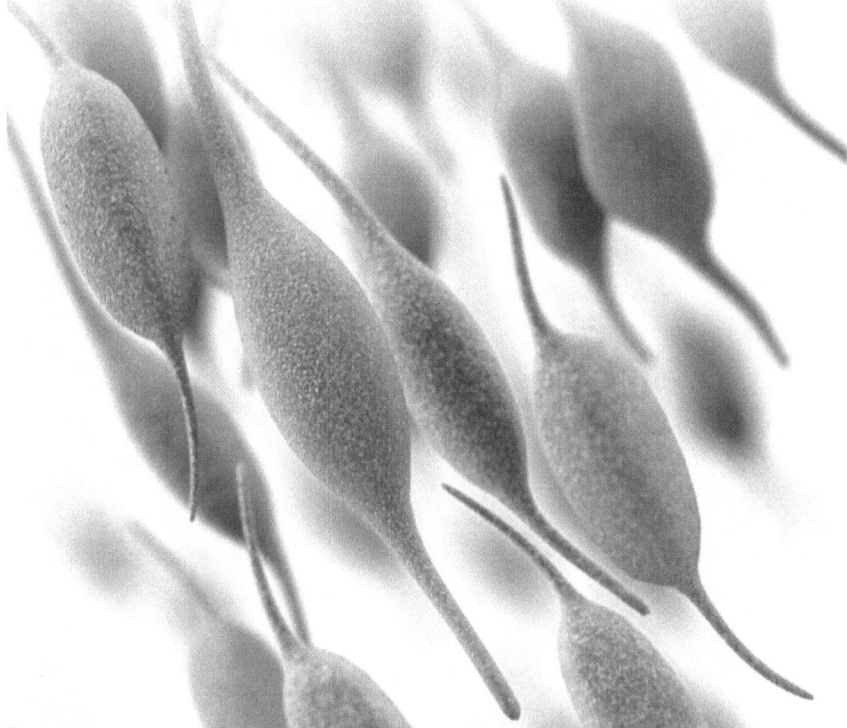

Figure i.1. Mycoplasma pneumoniae, bacteria. CDC, Sarah Bailey Cutchin

programming knowledge. The evolution of algorithms results in new possibilities for generative art.

Leonel Moura develops artwork based on the field of collective robotics. In the 2018 *Artists and Robots* show at the Grand Palais in Paris, his mechanisms employed sensors to avoid obstacles and detect colors, and a device to trigger a color marker pen. The robots would sense a color over which they passed, then reacted by either raising or lowering pens. The general behavior was inspired by a swarm of ants.[4]

Can audiences even distinguish between digital and human-created artwork? In June 2017, at the Eighth International Conference on Computational Creativity in Atlanta, the researchers reported that, on average, participants rated computer-generated artworks as being more novel, complex, and surprising than the paintings made by people. Their study found that 75% of the time, subjects incorrectly thought computer-created art was human created.[5]

Although the critical reaction is somewhat mixed, the commercial response to digital art is encouraging. Christie's in New York auctioned an artwork created by a computer entitled *Portrait of Edmond de Belamy*, which sold

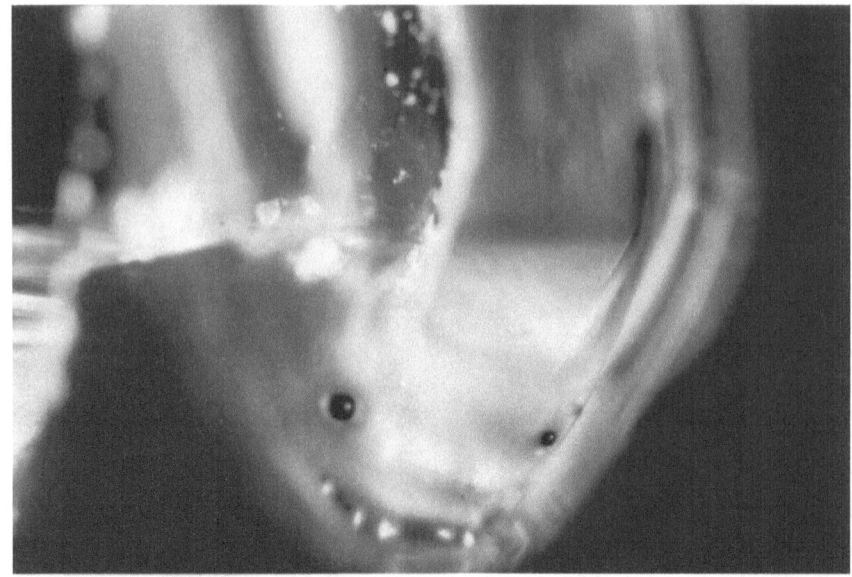

Figure i.2. Tissue Culture & Art Project. Oron Catts and Ionat Zurr

Figure i.3. Artbots at Work. Leonel Moura

for $432,500. The work is signed with the algorithm that created it. This sale was indicative of a growing interest in buying computer-generated art in traditional and non-traditional marketplaces.[6]

The emerging role of new technologies in biotechnology and artificial intelligence in various art disciplines is rarely explored except for in the unique publication *Leonardo*, the MIT-published periodical begun in the late 1960s with a broad focus on science, technology, and art. Otherwise, distributed information on the fusion of art and technology is scattered, at times technical, and in other instances concentrating on the strangeness of some of the creative products. There is little that considers the advancements in computer and biological art in the context of the broad field of aesthetics.

STARTING POINT

This book project started as an investigation into art and spirituality. For many artists in various traditions, creative artworks are attempts not only to characterize the human condition, but to connect with an elemental essence. Friedrich Nietzsche's *Birth of Tragedy* asserts the importance of the arts in spiritual terms: "Art is the highest task and the proper metaphysical activity of this life."[7] Nietzsche sees art as a deeply religious collective way of confronting existential dread, as evidenced in the Greek origins: "The Greek knew and felt the terror and horror of existence. That he might endure this terror at all, he had to interpose between himself and life the radiant dream-birth of the Olympians."[8]

Many experiencing the power of live performance can appreciate the idea of ancient Greek theater in which the whole free society took part in ritualistic, collective drama presented in monumental theaters. While every conscious creature feels the need for order in chaotic life, the intensity of this quest was exceptional in the Greeks. Their plays were an acting out of existential anxiety and an attempt to collectively manage it. I imagine Greek audiences peering at the performance on the stage as if it were a live, on-the-spot experiment where a truth might be discovered that indicated in some way what human existence is about.

When conducting the research for this book, the concentration on spirituality quickly turned to broader questions about consciousness, incarnation, and particular religious beliefs about the pervasiveness of beauty. Digital art and biological art forms rose to the forefront in pushing essential aesthetic definitions about beauty and agency. The artificial intelligence debate has been on my mind since first studying philosophy at the University of California, Berkeley, especially with the well-known philosopher Hubert L. Dreyfus, author of the provocative book *What Computers Can't Do: A Critique of*

Artificial Reason.[9] His lively seminars often centered on the importance of embodiment and cultural context in human intelligence. We will see later how the notion of embodiment still haunts discussions about machine intelligence.

It is important to note my perspective when writing about world culture. This book clearly comes from a Western perspective on aesthetics. As many scholars have pointed out when considering cross-cultural studies, and specifically global art forms, Western scholarship struggles to avoid inherent bias even in how questions are phrased about other cultures. As used in this book with its intrinsic limitations, non-Western culture is explored specifically in terms of artistic philosophies that may relate to biological, digital, and everyday aesthetic notions. There is no intention to present a comprehensive understanding of the vast research on non-Western art forms and traditions.

SHAPING QUESTIONS

The book is structured around these questions:

1. How might new computer and biological advancements affect our understanding of traditional aesthetics and artistic practice?
2. How does a knowledge of everyday aesthetics (pervasive creativity) positively affect us?

How Might New Computer and Biological Advancements Affect Our Understanding of Traditional Aesthetics and Artistic Practice?

In the philosophical field of aesthetics, the argument is often made that intellectual awareness or consciousness is a defining piece of art making. Art became philosophy in the 20th century with the contention that context, positioning, and attention are primary. In this way, any object in a frame placed in a museum or art gallery might be transformed into art by virtue of setting. Randomness, accident, and discovery in avant-garde art was a reaction to the traditional position.

Beyond context, many think that art doesn't require consciousness as much as process and interaction. They proclaim: No art, only artists. And further: No artists, only process. Some advocate for ego-less art, as seen in some forms of Eastern art. What might rapid technological advancements with learning machines and living organisms creating beautiful objects with varying degrees of human direction mean for artistic practice in the future?

Margaret Boden, a research professor in cognitive science, contends that our imagination can be liberated by a computational psychology:

> Now, at last, computational psychology is helping us to understand such things in scientific terms. It does this without lessening our wonder, or our self-respect, in any way. On the contrary, it increases them, by showing how extraordinary is the ordinary person's mind.[10]

In this way computer and biological art can strongly impact a discussion of aesthetics.

How Does a Knowledge of Everyday Aesthetics (Pervasive Creativity) Positively Affect Us?

In modern societies, artistic practice is often seen as an elite activity requiring unique talents and training with only the best resulting in placement in museums or on professional stages. Yet the distinction between fine art and other human forms of elaboration would be lost on most in the history of civilizations. How might an expanded view of art add to and complement what has been known as high and fine art to make it more powerful and accessible to all in daily life?

While there are differences in how individuals engage in the fine arts, there are commonalities regarding how we engage beauty throughout our daily lives. When we appreciate beauty, we tend to be more open, defenseless, and released from expected roles. One way to find more beauty in life suggested by some is a matter of attention, lengthening time by listening closely and looking for longer.

There are common challenges in pursuing an aesthetic life. First, an appreciation of beauty is easily pushed aside by the distractions and thoughts that everyday life brings us. Often beauty is regarded as a synonym for frivolity. Most importantly, throwing oneself completely into an aesthetic world is frightening for some because it involves a degree of suspension of the ego. In beauty we tend to forget ourselves.

A great deal is garnered by better understanding notions of beauty across cultures. For instance, in contrast to Western traditions, Eastern aesthetics suggests that ordered structures in art are contrived, and that linear thinking limits creativity. Many Japanese writers prize a quality of indecision in the structure of their work. Generally, Japanese aesthetics is more concerned with process than with product.

Japanese culture is structured with its aesthetic values at the center. Art is practiced as a way of life. What the Japanese eye seeks is the beauty of imperfection, or the "art of odd numbers." No other country has pursued the art of imperfection as eagerly as Japan.

The Japanese Zen style is to focus on one thing and search for the "sacred" within it. According to a Shinto saying, "Even in one single leaf on a tree, or in one blade of grass, the awesome deity presents itself." Japanese aesthetics displays some parallels to the British romantics and the American transcendentalists. Wordsworth and Coleridge inspired and stimulated their readers to use imagination to see the beauty in the everyday by praising commonplace happenings and changing them into a form of art. As William Blake wrote:

> To see a World in a Grain of Sand
> And a Heaven in a Wild Flower:
> Hold Infinity in the palm of your hand
> And Eternity in an hour. . . . [11]

In the Navajo world, art is integrated with everyday life. The creation of and incorporation of oneself in beauty represents the highest attainment and ultimate destiny of humans. Indeed, nearly all Navajos are artists and spend a large part of their time in artistic creation. Art is not an abstract quality; it is the normal pattern of nature and the most desirable form of experience.

We will see that the relatively new academic field of everyday aesthetics suggests creatively using and transforming the daily world through the illumination of those aspects of our lives that are normally neglected or ignored. More careful attention and a different mindset can reveal a surprisingly rich aesthetic dimension to the otherwise mundane. As Yuriko Saito at the Rhode Island School of Design notes:

> I think it is a mistake to limit what counts as the legitimate ingredients of everyday life for everyday aesthetics discourse: life does not come in neat packages of different experiences and everyday aesthetics should embrace its complexities with all the messiness created by them.[12]

She points out that common and ordinary human activities need to be illuminated or made unfamiliar to be aesthetically appreciated—there is really no such thing as art, only artists.

PLAN FOR THE BOOK

The book starts with the origin and evolution of European and American aesthetics, its philosophical foundations, spirituality and art, contemporary aesthetics, and psychological perspectives. *Aesthetic* derives from the

Greek *aesthesis*, meaning "perception" or "sensation." Beauty is perceived and sensed.

Beginning with the early Greek philosophers, Plato is generally critical of the arts, seeing them as perpetuating illusions. In Plato's world conception, human daily life itself is a mirage, merely shadows on the wall, murky impressions of the truth. The arts in general are seen by Plato as far removed from true reality and wisdom. Conversely, for Aristotle, art is imitation: His concentration is on realism—for instance, he asserts the superiority of portraits over simple color combination in art.

Both philosophers were heavily influenced by the ubiquitous and culturally central public theater practiced in Greece. The Greek chorus was originally the core of these performances, with a deeply religious purpose showing, through dancing and singing, human control unique in an unpredictable world. The long association of spirituality, mysticism, and religious traditions to art is traced, along modern and contemporary understandings of spirituality and art. In recent years, there has been a renewed interest in spirituality or meaning making in the art world, especially as seen in modern and contemporary art.

The arts have always been integral to religion. Sacred pictures, symbols, dances, chants, and hymns have been used in rituals, in places of worship, and as aids to prayer and meditation in virtually every religion. Judging by this alone, the arts seem to be natural vehicles for expressing or connecting with the transcendent. Even religions such as Judaism and Islam, which at times have considered images of God idolatrous, use striking designs to embellish places of worship and sacred texts.

Outside of formal religious contexts, spirituality has traditionally been as integral to the arts as to the rest of culture. The arts in traditional cultures transmit the central beliefs and values of those cultures, and those beliefs and values have a strong religious or spiritual dimension. The connection between art and mysticism is notable in many of the pioneers of modern abstract art at the beginning of the 20th century.

Chapter 2 investigates worldwide aesthetics starting with the anthropological foundations, and then cross-cultural patterns around the themes of disinterestedness, spirituality and transcendence, imperfection and process, and everyday beauty. The aesthetic preoccupation according to many scholars is a result of evolution, in which it became a selective advantage to create and appreciate innovation. Creating something is recognizing and looking closely, seeing what is new and special in things. In this way, appreciating the beautiful is a human evolutionary advantage.

Non-Western aesthetics often emphasize ego-less art making, which leads to transcendence. Such aesthetic approaches are often more concerned with process than with product, with construction rather than self-expression. The notion of imperfection is contextualized within a broad appreciation of the complex, varied, and constantly changing world.

Chapter 3 turns to contemporary notions of the aesthetics of the everyday and critical influences, especially John Dewey. The chapter outlines this field referring to the possibility of aesthetic experience of non-art objects and events. This movement within the field of philosophy of art rejects distinctions such as those between fine and popular art, art and craft, and aesthetic and non-aesthetic experiences.

The fourth chapter explores the fascinating developments in digital art. Digital art broadly defined is any artistic work or practice that uses digital technology as part of the creative process. Digital art can be purely computer-generated or taken from other sources. Digital art has been used in a variety of visual and performing arts, and in new forms such as NFTs (non-fungible tokens).

György Kepes at MIT led the way after World War II in combining art and technology. He wrote about the groundbreaking work of combining art and technology: "Our potent new tools, both conceptual and physical, contain within themselves an important aspect of these perspectives. For the more powerful devices we develop through our scientific technology, the more we are interconnected, interacting, interwoven with each other, with our machines, with our environment, and with our own inner capacities."[13]

Evolving from early experiments based at Bell Laboratories, MIT, and other research centers, the field exploded with developments in artificial intelligence. Questions of computer tools versus collaborators arise in the work of many artists and researchers in this field. The staggering progress made in artificial intelligence in creating written and visual pieces from simple text prompts is showing the way to the future and testing the exclusiveness of human ownership of art.

Chapter 5 turns to the world of biological art involving the appreciation of nature, as well as the actual artistic control of living organisms. Beginning with the early genetic manipulation of plants for artistic ends, the field is powered by tools that allow humans to see micro and macro natural worlds never viewed before, and through biotechnology artists now creating and directing organisms for artistic ends.

Finally, in the conclusion, primary contrasts between traditional and transformative aesthetics are summarized, and implications for individuals and institutions considered. The book ends by briefly contemplating strategies for living more fulfilling aesthetic lives.

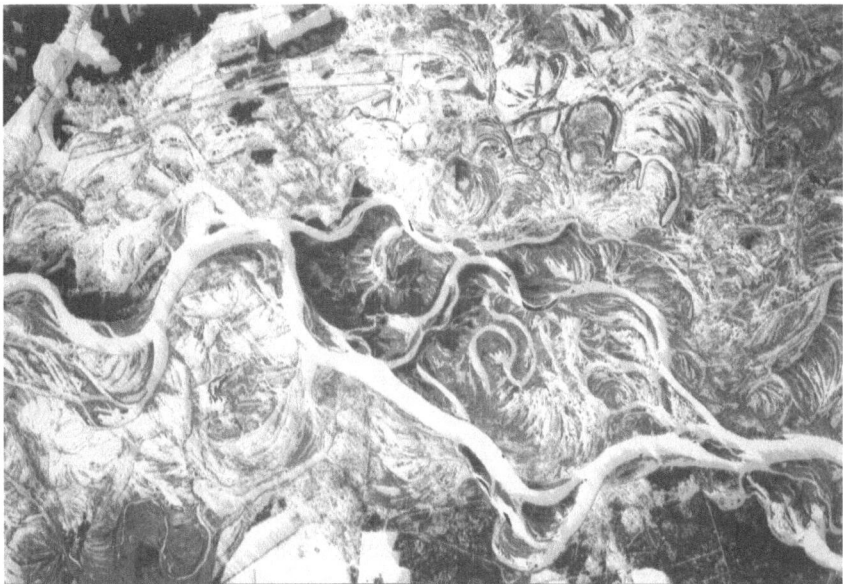

Figure i.4. *The Frozen Wild Dnieper River.* NASA, Curling snow drifts are magnified by the terrain around the 1,400-mile Dnieper River, flowing from Russia to the Black Sea in this image from the International Space Station on February 9, 2017.

CONCLUSION

Understanding beauty is essential to our lives. The arts have the power to elicit deep emotions in all. Whether or not one identifies these feelings as spiritual or a heightened mental state, the power of art from earliest times comes from its evocative force. This book considers how the work of artists is a form of existential exploration, and how we can all benefit by living creative lives.

According to William James, transcendent moments—beautiful, sublime, divine—often occur after great personal upheaval, disrupting our habitual frames of perception. James called these moments "pure experience." Many find solace in nature and think about the contrast with that found in human works of art. John Dewey contended that experience is itself aesthetic, and art is the consummation of ordinary experience found everywhere.

In recent years, there has been renewed interest in spirituality and meaning making in the art world. At museums worldwide, artists such as Hilma af Klint and Agnes Pelton, who deeply explore mysticism and religion, are gaining attention. This growing interest around meaning and faith systems is apparent in the work of contemporary artists and explicitly discussed in relation to new approaches to digital, biological, and everyday art.

Challenges to the rather limited scope of aesthetics restricted to highbrow arts and the detailing of the characteristics of the beautiful began during the latter half of the 20th century with a renewed interest in nature and the environment. The emerging field of the familiar or everyday aesthetics, particularly represented in the work of Yuriko Saito, continues this trajectory of widening the scope of the field of aesthetics to including objects, events, and activities that constitute daily life.

As detailed in my previous book, *A Career in the Arts: The Complex Learning and Career Needs of Creative Professionals*,[14] those pursuing careers in the visual and performing arts face many well-documented social challenges beyond the technical demands of each field. Overcoming racism, sexism, and agism is clearly one piece of the opening of the arts to a more diverse population. A less-understood aspect of the challenge to democratize the arts is the insight into the way in which everyone, every day, is touched by art in ways that aren't generally appreciated. This book explores how we gain by understanding ways to live imaginative lives and considers the increasingly important collaborative role of computers and interaction with nature.

NOTES

1. Csikszentmihalyi, M. (1996). *Creativity: Flow and the psychology of discovery and invention*. New York: HarperCollins, p. 318.

2. https://tcaproject.net/ ; Catts, O., & Zurr, I. (2002). Growing semi-living sculptures: The tissue culture art project. *Leonardo*, 35(4): 365–70. doi: https://doi.org/10.1162/002409402760181123.

3. Blaise Agüera, y. A. (2017). Art in the age of machine intelligence†. *Arts*, 6(4): 18. doi:https://doi.org/10.3390/arts6040018.

4. Moura, L. (2018). Robot art: An interview with Leonel Moura. *Arts*, 7(3): 28–. https://doi.org/10.3390/arts7030028.

5. Elgammal, A., Liu, B., Elhoseiny, M., & Mazzone, M. (2017). Can: Creative adversarial networks, generating "art" by learning about styles and deviating from style norms. arXiv preprint arXiv:1706.07068.

6. Miller, A.I. (2019). *The artist in the machine: The world of AI-powered creativity*. Cambridge, MA: MIT Press ; www.theguardian.com/technology/2019/mar/04/can-machines-be-more-creative-than-humans.

7. Nietzsche, F. (1927). *The philosophy of Nietzsche*. New York: The Modern Library, p. 950.

8. Nietzsche, F. (1927). *The philosophy of Nietzsche*. New York: The Modern Library, p. 962.

9. Dreyfus, H.L. (1972). *What computers can't do: A critique of artificial reason*. New York: Harper & Row.

10. Boden, M.A. (2004). *The creative mind: Myths and mechanisms.* London, UK: Routledge, p. 303–304.

11. Blake, William. Extract from "Auguries of innocence."

12. Saito, Y. (2017). *Aesthetics of the familiar: Everyday life and world-making.* Oxford, UK: Oxford University Press, p. 11.

13. Smithsonian Institution Archives. Record Unit 333, Box 9, Folder: Explorations, p. 36.

14. Berg, G.A. (2022). *A career in the arts: The complex learning and career needs of creative professionals.* New York: Rowman & Littlefield.

Chapter 1

The Origin and Evolution of Western Aesthetics

We begin with a look at the philosophical foundations of the field of aesthetics, especially focused on Western traditions arising from ancient Greece. The discussion then turns to historical links between spirituality and art, conceptions of transcendence, as well as contemporary trends. Moving from religion to psychology, the role of the unconscious in the production of artistic works is considered.

PHILOSOPHICAL FOUNDATIONS

Scholars trace the Western origin of philosophical treatment of the arts and what would become aesthetics to ancient Greece in the writings of Plato and Aristotle. According to Plato, "The appeal of dramatic poetry is not to the reason but to a lower part, the emotions, which, like the senses, are subject to illusions."[1] As a political theorist, Plato was afraid of the irrational emotional power of the arts, and their power to tell convincing lies or subversive truths. He favored strict censorship and would banish the dramatists from his ideal state. Plato believed that art is hostile to religion as well as to philosophy—art is a sort of egoistic substitute for the preferred discipline of religion.[2]

On the other hand, for Aristotle, art was imitation:

> Imitation is natural to man from childhood, one of his advantages over the lower animals being this, that he is the most imitative creature in the world and learns at first by imitation. And it is also natural for all to delight in works of imitation.[3]

In addition to imitation, Aristotle focused on realism and dramatic action or plot. In drama, characterization comes second to the storyline. His concentration is on realism, for instance asserting the superiority of portraits over simple color combination in art: "The most beautiful colors laid on without order will not give one the same pleasure as a simple black-and-white sketch of a portrait."[4]

Aristotle contended that tragedy developed from epic poetry, not from religious practices honoring Dionysus. As opposed to Plato, Aristotle was preoccupied with facts, not myth and religion.[5] Nevertheless, the nebulous notion of "catharsis," meaning literally "a cleaning," was introduced by Aristotle into Western culture.

> A tragedy, then, is the imitation of an action that is serious and also, as having magnitude, complete in itself; in language with pleasurable accessories, each kind brought in separately in the parts of the work; in a dramatic, not in a narrative form; with incidents arousing pity and fear, wherewith to accomplish its catharsis of such emotions.[6]

Overall, Plato regarded Athenian drama as the most dangerous and corrupting of all forms of entertainment, while Aristotle praised it as the most complete and satisfying art.

The specifically Athenian institution of the satyr play, with choruses of men in costume, appeared at the very end of the 6th century BC. Based on archeological evidence gathered from vases and reliefs, it is believed the Greek chorus both sang and danced. The chorus was originally the core of popular public performances, with a reportedly deeply religious purpose expressed in dance and voice demonstrating perfect human control in an otherwise-unpredictable world. Only the vaguest idea of the music played is known. Choreography probably drew heavily upon older ritual dance, and the words sung by the chorus emphasized the power of the gods.[7]

Friedrich Nietzsche traced the role of the arts in early civilizations, through the Greeks, into modern times, and what he termed "Dionysian" emotions that cause self-forgetfulness. Nietzsche pointed to the Greek chorus as a central piece among early peoples to sustain a shared culture: "In song and in dance man expresses himself as a member of a higher community; he has forgotten how to walk and speak; he is about to take a dancing flight into the air His very gestures bespeak enchantment."[8] The result of participating in a performance is metaphysical comfort:

> Life at bottom is indestructible, powerful and pleasurable, appears with objective clarity as the satyr chorus, the chorus of natural beings, who as it were live ineradicably behind every civilization, and who, despite the ceaseless change of generations and the history of nations, remain the same to all eternity.[9]

Art is an effective "transfiguring mirror" for humans reflecting man's interpretation of life back on life: "The same impulse which calls art into being, as the complement and consummation of existence, seducing one to a continuation of life, was also the cause of the Olympian world which the Hellenic 'will' made use of as a transfiguring mirror."[10]

One scholar notes a deep-seated need to discover order in the flux of physical and psychological experience as a constant feature in ancient Greek artistic expression.

> While it is true that every conscious creature feels this need to some extent, the intensity with which the quest for order was carried on by the Greeks was exceptional. Whether as a result of some mysterious tendency in the national psyche, or as a spontaneous reaction to their turbulent historical experience after the break-up of the Mycenaean world, the Greeks felt that to live with changing, undefined, unmeasured, seemingly random impressions—to live, in short, with what was expressed by the Greek word *chaos*—was to live in a state of constant anxiety.[11]

The innate drive for order in this way may be an historical root of artistic practice.

According to R. G. Collingwood in *The Principles of Art*, the modern sense of the word *art* is relatively recent. The Greek word means a form of skill or a craft. In fact, the Greeks and Romans had no sense of art beyond craft. Renaissance artists also thought of themselves as craftsmen, and it was not until afterward when aesthetics and art separated, defined as fine art versus craft. By the 18th century, the fine arts were solidly linked to the beautiful, not to the merely crafted.[12]

The German philosopher Alexander Baumgarten is credited as the first to use the Greek term *aisthetikos*, which originally meant "pertaining to sense perception," and give it its modern meaning. Its goal is beauty, in contrast with logic, whose goal is truth. Aesthetics became a branch of philosophy defining beauty, how it is properly recognized and judged.

The word *aesthetic* has many uses. The most widely applied distinguishes the beautiful from the merely pleasing or useful. Perception and the senses are an important part of the basic principles of the aesthetic. Throughout this book, we will see how central the physical sensory aspect of beauty is to many different philosophical approaches, and the possible relevance to digital art.

Although a slippery term, there is some consensus from modern scholars on the essential characteristics of aesthetic experience. A lineage of British thinkers situates aesthetics at the center of their studies and develops a detailed and complex understanding of it. Notably, the author of *In the Art of Appreciation*, Harold Osborne, discusses eight specific features regarded as characteristic of the aesthetic attitude.

Some assert that aesthetics as a field suffered because of the institutional divide in Anglo-American humanities departments separating reflection on art and beauty from the rest of what was called Arts and Letters. This bifurcation is a product of the 18th century, which set aesthetics as a distinct branch of philosophy, and of the 19th-century university with its formation of distinct disciplines.[13]

It is important to note here regarding where aesthetic perceptions lie—it will come into play later in discussions about non-Western art and most importantly in digital art. Collingwood argues that the audience, not just the artist, encountering a work of art, has an aesthetic experience:

> If art is not a kind of craft, but the expression of emotion, this distinction of kind between artist and audience disappears. . . . Hence, when some one reads and understands a poem, he is not merely understanding the poet's expression of his, the poet's, emotions, he is expressing emotions of his own in the poet's words, which have thus become his own words. As Coleridge put it, we know a man for a poet by the fact that he makes us poets. We know that he is expressing his emotions by the fact that he is enabling us to express ours.[14]

Furthermore, Collingwood points to the role of consciousness in the aesthetic experience: "The activity which generates an artistic experience is the activity of consciousness."[15] This is a key point to keep in mind, especially when considering biological and digital art. What is the role of consciousness in art? Is beauty located in the artwork, the artist, and/or the viewer?

SPIRITUALITY AND ART

The long history of the association of art forms and spirituality in Western civilization reveals that the strong evocative nature of art viewed as a powerful way to reach an illiterate population. In addition to tracing the mostly Christian religious views of art, this section delves into the important notions of the sublime and the transcendent. These concepts get at the central function of art in spiritual growth. Finally, the close association between modern art and spirituality is considered.

Religious Traditions and Art

The history of Christianity displays periods of disdain and appreciation of art. The Bible is rich in imagery, and in ancient times both Jews and Christians adorned their places of worship with visual depictions drawn from holy texts. When the believer views an icon, it is a look through a window into the world of religious mysteries. Only the early persecution of Christians in the Roman Empire restrained the visual arts from flourishing.[16]

In the Christian spiritual tradition, beauty and goodness were for centuries inseparably linked.[17] The King James Version of the Old Testament associates beauty and the Lord: "One thing have I desired of the LORD, that will I seek after; that I may dwell in the house of the LORD all the days of my life, to behold the beauty of the LORD, and to enquire in his temple."[18] Art manifests the beauty and the attractiveness of the divine, also manifested in nature. The Wisdom of Solomon declares that "from the greatness and beauty of created things comes a corresponding perception of their Creator."[19]

However, at times Christianity viewed the seduction of visual images and music as like the pagan immorality displayed in certain Roman and Greek practices. Playing the lyre specifically was associated with prostitution.[20]

Although Western Christian thinkers tended to be anxious about the potential of artistic images to mislead, early theologians also recognized the power of images to complement verbal truths. In the eighth and ninth centuries, the Iconoclastic Controversy arose about the use of images in Christian worship. The dispute was eventually settled in favor of the use of some illustrations, although Reformed theologians (notably Calvin) continued to disapprove. Calvin, as with Augustine, saw the problem in that any intense desire toward the visible loveliness of the world distracts from intellectual and interior contemplation for which true piety constantly aspires. Calvin's iconoclasm is a major feature of the Protestant Reformation and the critique of images.[21]

The Council of Trent insisted that images were only to be venerated, not adored. Artists were put on notice that the seductions of the world and depictions of the holy belonged to different spheres. "Thou shalt not make to thyself any graven image, nor the likeness of anything that is in heaven above, or in the earth beneath, or in the water under the earth. Thou shalt not bow down to them, nor worship them."[22] Nevertheless, thereafter the use of images in art was generally thought to be strategic in making spiritual truth accessible to those who could not read.[23]

Martin Luther's influence on Western religious attitudes toward the arts is significant. While beauty is not a major theme in Luther's work, it is crucial in shaping the question of who God, Christ, and humans are. Like many at the time, Luther is critical of Catholicism's specific use of images as moneymaking objects. An example of this critical perspective on the use of iconography is seen in Martin Luther's comment upon viewing extravagant relics at Saint Peter's Basilica in the early 16th century, whereupon he reportedly said it was "built with the flesh, skin, and bones of the flock."[24]

Medieval thinkers list proportion, color, and integrity as valid indicators of beauty, while Luther viewed such matters as hidden. God's beauty, Christ's beauty, and human beauty in Christ is concealed to human eyes and grasped only by faith. According to Luther, secular views of beauty are inadequate because they fail to account for the wonder and mystery that people experience.

In contrast to contemporary aesthetics, which some analysts contend has a hard time discerning a wider purpose to life and the world, gospel beauty is said to permit believers to feel at home in the world. One of the most treasured hymns of American Lutherans is "Beautiful Savior." To associate beauty with Jesus Christ is part of the Lutheran identity, encoded within the doctrine of justification by grace alone through faith.[25]

Music was central to Luther's views of the arts. For Luther, music was a creation of God and a gift whereby God shapes humans. The gift is given precisely for human enjoyment, an "innocent pleasure." Creating music makes humans vessels of beauty. The beauty of music happens in the interplay between order and freedom, "simplicity" and "sweetness," which Luther understood as the core of music.[26]

For most of the Christian world, the use of images in art was important in making spiritual truth accessible to those who could not read. If human beings are in some respect images of God, then the use of icons assists in the process of restoration by becoming more Christlike. Spirituality is the process by which the divine spirit changes followers into the image and likeness of Christ.[27]

Umberto Eco notes that people of the Middle Ages thought of symbols as real and a way of communicating directly with God.[28] Symbolistic art operates beyond form, with God revealing himself to man in physical form. Masks, too, proclaim God's presence in the everyday world. By means of masks, the dead in a sense return to life.[29]

Medieval thinkers of various schools tend to associate beauty with goodness. For some, this is because both goodness and beauty were "transcendentals" describing the structure of being. The theology of beauty developed in the Middle Ages was deeply informed by philosophical views stemming from the ancient Greeks, especially Plato. The three criteria for beauty defined by Thomas Aquinas—proportion, light or color, and integrity or perfection—find their roots in Plato's thinking.[30]

Medieval scholars debate traits to include on the list of transcendentals, also seen as other names for God. That list generally includes being, oneness, and truth, along with goodness. Beauty is sometimes placed on that list.[31]

The sacralization of art took shape from the late 18th century to the end of the 19th century, when Romantic writers and artists asserted that art and nature could produce a bracing experience of what is variously called the infinite, the sublime, the timeless, or the divine. "Artists were geniuses who had access to such domains and needed to be championed against the incursions of bourgeois sensibility, orthodox religion, false taste, and the state."[32]

Paracelsus, a 16th-century philosopher, argued that God gave humans the beauty of nature to gain knowledge of Him, and this splendor was embodied in the working processes of craftspeople. The art of the craftsman "reformed" nature, creating noble objects from the dross of fallen nature. In this way, invisible knowledge is made discernible.[33] According to the *Astronomia Magna* by Paracelsus, "God wishes that the things that are invisible should become visible."

Since aesthetics was not established as a formal discipline until the mid-18th century, the arts were a form of craftsmanship, and beauty was understood metaphysically. For medieval thinkers, beauty was an attribute of God.[34]

The quickening of global commerce and the rise of urban noble courts opened a space for artisans and practitioners to assert themselves. As they became economically more powerful, they began to show a consciousness of their own productive power and claimed a new intellectual and social authority for themselves based on their relationship to nature.[35]

The Sublime and Transcendence

The sublime is an aesthetic concept originating in ancient Greece, and it plays a particularly important part in 18th-century writing about art. It is a category of aesthetic experience associated with ideas of awe and vastness held to be distinct from the beautiful. The key work on the concept of the sublime in English was Edmund Burke's 1757 *A Philosophical Enquiry into the Origin of our Ideas of the Sublime and Beautiful*, which identified the power of suggestion to stimulate the imagination. The forces through which this concept functions in the spheres of human experience are transcendence and the unrepresentable.[36]

The spell of the sublime makes us believe that the unrepresentable is somehow truer than the representable. This is an ancient preoccupation and belief that art reaches beyond our immediate circumstances. Transcendence has become a key concept in the contemporary talk of theology and the arts.

The notion that great art is not of this world is something that artists themselves often talk about. The arts serve as unique and compelling witnesses to the fact that the finite world we inhabit always exceeds our grasp, always outstrips our representations of it. There is a fullness or plenitude of meaning in the world that is inexhaustible, that outperforms our perception. "In short, they can remind us that we are not God."[37]

In modern times, there is a strong link between God as creator and the work of artists. Yet in Christian antiquity and most of the medieval era, the term *creator* was reserved for God, not humans. Only God truly created. In this way, creativity became the making of new things, not creating out of nothing, as God does.

The historical definition of *mysticism* has to do with the direct intuition or experience of God. A mystic is a person who has this experience. Mystical encounters bring serenity or bliss. Such events may have some relation to the spontaneous experience of the unity of the world and with certain kinds of chemical- and drug-induced incidents, but the connections are much disputed.[38]

Some comment on the link between spirituality and ecstatic states through the vehicle of the gospel choir, and the original ecstatic structure of the Judeo-Christian service. Ecstatic states are created in the surrender to a higher system of organization. In this merged state, mystical experiences occur.[39]

Stephen James Newton, in his book *Painting, Psychoanalysis, and Spirituality*, distinguished between two fundamental types of form: conscious and inarticulate. The inarticulate is an accidental by-product of the creative process orchestrated by an artist. He contended that religious icon painting is vested in the transformative and transcendent experiences of ecstasy. The icon offers access to what is essentially another spatial and temporal dimension. It is a psychic experience. For Newton, this fact explains much of the animosity toward visual art and religious iconography.[40]

Viacheslav Ivanov, one of the most prominent Russian symbolist poets at the beginning of the 20th century and a leading theorist, understood art as one of the most effective forms of contact between human beings and the spiritual world. He differentiated three "aesthetic principles" of the universe, which all together constitute the beautiful—the sublime, beauty, and the chaotic—and linked them to the three stages of being of the artist in the process of creative activity. The artist first passes through the subconscious stage of demonic chaos.

Next, the artist undergoes the process of ascent into the ideal, spiritual sphere, where he gains inexpressible experience. After that, the process of the descent of the artist toward the earth takes place, where artists attempt to express in the form of artistic symbols the experience they have acquired.[41] According to Ivanov, both the symbol and its content, myth, are of divine origin—they are "embodiments of the divine truth." Therefore, high art is one of the principal ways of one's ascent to spiritual reality by means of sensory reality.[42]

Modern and Contemporary Scholars on Art and Spirituality

Religious organizations foster connections between spirituality and the arts. One national study found that 38% of religious organizations sponsor choral singing and 24% offer other performing arts activities such as dance, instrumental music, or theater.[43] Furthermore, the great increase of interest in the links between art and religion has led to emphasis on the complex experiential aspects of religion instead of on traditional organizations. Large numbers of Americans are potentially exposed to spirituality (broadly defined) through the arts by participating, at least casually, in some form of the arts. In several ways the modern museum replicates formal religious devotion in revealing a higher reality.[44]

In national data, 20% of artists say they currently have no religious preference, significantly more than in the public at large, where 8% give that response. American artists are often characterized as experimenting with one religious idea after another. However, one scholar argues there is a difference between a deep religious search, and a kind of consumerism or shopping for spiritualism. Many artists are drawn to artistic careers because of personal trauma and/or disruption in their families. Subsequent personal reflection is facilitated by artistic practice and leads to new perspectives on life.[45]

Although many modern artists conceive of their art as an avenue of search for deep meaning, the culture at large in the 20th century was unreceptive to the spiritual aspect of artists' work.[46] Instead, the century was dominated by science and material progress so that metaphysics was generally absent from popular discussion. Some scholars note that spirituality seems to be in fashion once again, but in a new pragmatic sense:

> Not the Christian sort necessarily, although charismatic evangelicals are enjoying a resurgence. The search for enlightenment is just as likely to lead to the ancient faiths of the East or the latest New Age cult from California. For it is a search with a difference. The question is no longer "Is it true?" but "Does it work?" One of the things that seem to work is art.[47]

The notion that art and spirituality are complementary would have been treated with skepticism earlier, when art for art's sake was the prevailing attitude. By the end of the 20th century, the idea of art and spirituality became more popular, starting perhaps as notably seen in the 1986 LACMA and the *Gemeentemuseum in The Hague* joint exhibit, "The Spiritual in Art: Abstract Painting 1880–1985." Contemporary views of spirituality and art move in multiple directions at once from a reaction against the spirituality and art viewpoint, to the continued expansion of what is meant by art.[48]

Key modern thinkers about art and religion are led by Paul Tillich, who developed the field of the theology and the arts, often a regular part of contemporary undergraduate theology programs. His contribution was in moving beyond religious content to form and process. For Tillich, genuine art expressed a particular moment of human self-interpretation grounded in a breakthrough expressing the presence of God prior to any knowledge of Him.

Tillich identified three elements of style: form, *Inhalt*, and *Gehalt*. As an expression of culture, the *Inhalt* is the content and *Gehalt* is its significance. In this way, there is a "sacredness" in great art. Tillich urges us to view religion not as a separate component of human existence, but rather as the dimension of depth in all human endeavors.[49]

The 20th-century French philosopher Simone Weil believed that art seeks to make evident "the infinite beauty of the entire universe." Unlike Plato, she asserted that rather than seek the real beyond the material, we must instead strip ourselves of the illusion that we are at the center of the universe, in effect taking the place of God. This renunciation of self allows us to be transformed inwardly by what we look at.

Key elements of abstract art link to spirituality such as the idea of analogy, acknowledgment of the primary force of the image itself, and a concept of the inner life as possessing multiple levels. Some recent scholars suggest looking at Christian art in a process of unselfing and sacrifice. For advocates of non-objective art, the form starts where representational art leaves off and has the advantage of not wrestling with figurative elements and instead concentrating on spiritual ones. The form is said to look beyond visible nature and presents its animating forces in the process of creation.[50]

Some scholars argue that the defining characteristic of contemporary art culture is irony.

> Borrow from wherever you feel like, but don't take anything too seriously. Make any statement you like, but make sure your tongue is firmly in your cheek. You can't believe politicians, preachers or even post-modern philosophers, so send them up. Values are passe, so are strong emotions.[51]

This ironic positioning of the artist makes holding religious beliefs problematic.

Others contend that imagining religion is pervasive in contemporary art may come from a lack of religious literacy generally: "A specter is haunting contemporary art—the specter of religion."[52]

Suzi Gablik in *The Re-Enchantment of Art* claims that contemporary culture has lost the capacity for meaningful ritual:

> One of the peculiar developments in our Western world is that we are losing our sense of the divine side of life, of the power of imagination, myth, dream and vision. The particular structure of modern consciousness, centered in a rationalizing, abstracting and controlling ego determines the world we live in and how we perceive and understand it; without the magical sense of perception, we do not live in a magical world.[53]

She defines the task of the "re-enchantment project" as developing a more open model of the psyche so that as a culture we can reclaim the power and importance of vision through the remythologizing of consciousness through art and ritual. Art has the power to re-humanize and re-enchant.

Ken Gire, as quoted in Robert K. Johnston's *The Film Viewer and Natural Theology: God's Presence at the Movies*, talks about the power of film to provide moments of transcendence:

> I have experienced [God] . . . more in movie theaters than I have in churches. Why? I can't say for sure . . . movies don't always tell the truth, don't always enlighten, don't always inspire. What they do on a fairly constant basis is give you an experience of transcendence.

Others contend that exercising and extreme running is a spiritual practice:

> Today's ultrarunners are literal ascetic athletes who engage in extreme, meaningful bodily experiences and practices very similar to the ascetics. Ultrarunning has a distinct spiritual dimension that lends itself to solitude and reflection, and is a kind of embodied spiritual practice that one author calls "ultrarunning spirituality."[54]

Stephen Pattison in "Response to Re-enchantment and Art Discussion" contends that discussions of art and religion need to be contextualized more firmly in the complex phenomenology of interactions in which people find meaning in everyday life. This is often done through the medium of various kinds of everyday artifacts outside of typical formal artistic contemplation. He suggests that "maybe the world is just differently enchanted, not disenchanted."[55] In Chapter 3, where the topic of everyday aesthetics is discussed, a similar argument is made.

MODERN AESTHETICS

Modern aesthetics outside the religious realm moved in multiple directions, continuing various Western traditions, influenced by a greater understanding of Eastern approaches to the arts. At the same time, the appreciation of what had been known as "primitive art" combined with the attack by artists themselves on the very notion of what is considered "art" led to what some have claimed was its downfall.

Arthur Danto famously announced the extinction of art based on two major historical changes. First, the invention of photography and motion pictures meant the capacity for illusion passed entirely outside of the hands of painters, and second, the understanding in the late 19th century of the artistic merit of primitive art contradicted the narrative of Western art superiority.

More precisely, Danto claimed not that art was dead, but that it had turned into philosophy.

> But once art makers are freed from the task of finding the essence of art, which had been thrust upon art at the inception of Modernism, they too have been liberated from history, and have entered the era of freedom. Art does not stop with the end of art history. What happens only is that one set of imperatives has been lifted from its practice as it enters what I think of as its posthistorical phase.[56]

Artphilohistocritisophory is the term Danto invented to describe the historical moment in art in which artists, art historians, teachers, philosophers, and critics became so interlocked in one another's activities that the making of any artwork whatsoever demanded a complex philosophical justification supplied by the artist. Danto credits Hans Belting, along with himself, for bringing forward the idea of the end of art but argues they were really describing a further evolution of the form: "Neither Belting nor I was claiming that art had stopped or that it was going to stop, but only that in whatever way it was going to go on, that would be consistent with its having come to an end."[57]

According to Danto, there were three distinct stages in the history of art. Art was, for most of its history, guided by the imitation theory of art advocated by Aristotle. The second brief stage was guided by defining art as an expression of feelings. The final stage of the philosophical history of art is characterized by the theory that anything can be an artwork. The function of an artwork came to simply be reflect on the nature of art.[58]

In this way, by the mid-1960s, Danto argued that artists questioned the very foundation of fine art. The pervasiveness of photography, film, and video media in particular rendered art obsolete as a medium of imitation, as Aristotle had contended. The subsequent non-mimetic art was historically an admission of the form's demise. Thus, the self-conscious question of defining what art is became the central preoccupation for many artists[59]

Finally, Danto argued for a distinction between art and real objects:

> The artworld stands to the real world in something like the relationship in which the City of God stands to the Earthly City. Certain objects, like certain individuals, enjoy a double citizenship, but there remains, the RT notwithstanding, a fundamental contrast between artworks and real objects."[60]

Another well-known critic, Donald Kuspit, in his book *The End of Art*, contended that to see works of art in a non-aesthetic way is to return them to the state in which they existed before they were recognized or realized as works of art. He coins the term *postart* for this counter-aesthetic movement and critically attacks it:

It takes its triviality far too seriously to be self-subversive. It suggests that the conceptual postartist is the most banal entertainer of all, for he "performs" completely banal ideas. . . . He has absolutely no interest in aesthetics and lacks the craft necessary to create beauty.[61]

For Kuspit, what used to be thought of as high art in postart loses whatever uncommon qualities made it far from ordinary. In this way, postart's role is to convince us that no other experience is possible than daily experience:

Postart is completely banal art—unmistakably everyday art, neither kitsch nor high art, but an in-between art that glamorizes everyday reality while pretending to analyze it. Postart claims to be critical of everyday reality but in fact is unwittingly collusive with it.[62]

Kuspit looks further at the performance aspect of postart and events known as "happenings" occurring in the late 20th century. He contends that the postart happening is understood to be just another daily event and attempts to turn non-art milieus into artistic ones, as if all daily life is something special. "Performance art is the dominant form—even essence—of postart, which in principle began with the move away from object making to quasi-theatrical action similar to that occurring in Dadaism and Futurism."[63]

Performance art brings together art and life, and site-based work frees art from the stigma of being an illusion. We will see later in the examination of the emerging field of everyday aesthetics congruencies with Kuspit's notion of postart. His objection to glamorizing the ordinary and banal is one critics have consistently leveled against this strain of aesthetics.

Environmental aesthetics is yet another one of the major areas of aesthetics to have emerged in the second half of the 20th century. It originated as a reaction to the emphasis on fine art in aesthetics, concentrating instead on the enjoyment of natural environments. The scope of environmental aesthetics has broadened to include not simply natural environments, but also human-influenced and human-constructed ones.

The discipline has also come to include the examination of things within environments, giving rise to the aesthetics of everyday life. This area involves the beauty of common objects and environments, as well as a range of everyday activities. The original philosophical developments in the aesthetics of nature occurred in the 18th century, when the founders of modern philosophy began to take nature rather than art as the definitive art object. At the same time, they also developed the concept of disinterestedness as a chief characteristic of such experience.[64]

A ramification of the environmental approach is that human environments becomes closely aligned with the aesthetics of art. Since human environments are conceived of as deliberately designed, they are regarded as akin to works of art, and all the theories, conceptions, and assumptions about the philosophy of art are brought in.[65]

Twentieth-century philosophers such as Iris Murdoch often concentrate on the practical impact of aesthetic experience. Central to Murdoch's thought about art is the strangeness, the solitude, the psychological and social risks inherent in the "examined life." She claims that art is dangerous play with unconscious forces and that we enjoy art because it disturbs us in deep, often incomprehensible ways.[66]

Murdoch argues that art is good for people precisely because it breaks the grip of our own dull fantasy life and stirs us to the effort of true vision. She claims that most of the time we fail to see the real world at all because we are blinded by obsession and anxiety contained within a small personal realm. Great art is liberating, enabling us to see and take pleasure in what is not ourselves. For Murdoch, the essence of the power of art is a "love" of something other than oneself.[67]

PSYCHOLOGICAL PERSPECTIVES

Modern art and psychoanalysis developed in tandem in the late 19th century, and both are concerned with what lies in the unconscious. Most psychoanalytic interpretations of artworks view them as if they are dreams. Freud saw art as a sublimation involving the substitute gratification of unconscious instinctive desire, and therefore an artist was something of a neurotic. On the other hand, Jung practiced art regularly himself and used it as a tool to understand unconscious symbolism.

According to Jungian psychology, the human personality has four aspects, or functions, set in two opposing pairs. The first pair is thinking and feeling, and the second pair is intuition and sensation. The first pair is rational, the second irrational. Johnson, following Jung, contends that one can enter a conversation with the different parts of oneself that live in the unconscious. In this model, the imagination is neither the conscious nor the unconscious, but rather what lies between the two.[68]

Carl Jung differentiated between the conventional artist, who deals only with conscious, "given" contents accepted by society (or a social group), and the visionary artist, who is taken over by some immense force arising from the unconscious. Some argue that genuine religious art evokes this deeper contemplation in us—if we are willing to search until it triggers some inner realizations—and in many cases it confronts while it inspires.[69]

In *Principles of Psychology*, William James, the American founder of psychology, developed a model of selfhood that has at its center the material self, and then the social self. Finally, there is the spiritual self, one that is sought or experienced in "intellectual, moral, and religious aspiration." This is the farthest reaching, but also the most subtle and easily neglected. According to Kaag, James hoped there was something ethereal and transcendent free from the constraints of our physical lives. "At many times throughout his life, he suggested that one can occasionally feel this 'something' haunting the fringe of consciousness."[70]

James, in his chapter on stream of consciousness in *Principles of Psychology*, argues that we sleepwalk through life, operating well below our experiential thresholds in a preparatory step, setting the conditions for us to become aware that the stream of consciousness and its ceaseless flow. Sometimes simply attending to the edges and breaks of experience is enough to bring on a coming to consciousness. James claims that transcendent moments can occur after, or during, great personal turmoil.

> In truth, I suspect tragedy and turmoil have the unintended consequence of disrupting our habitual frames of perception, the instrumental ways that we typically interpret the world, just long enough for what James later called "pure experience."[71]

On the margins of a section of text manuscript that addresses the elusiveness of the stream of consciousness, James wrote a single phrase, "The Witness," to describe a detached, yet involved perspective that perceives the unfolding of things as one sees them. James suggests in his later writings that immersing oneself in the stream of consciousness, and orienting oneself to its mystery, could save a life: "We are born into a uniquely compromised position—somewhere between amoebas and angels—but we have the chance to work through it."[72]

The scholar John Kaag takes an interesting approach in writing about James from a contemporary aesthetic position. In *Sick Souls, Healthy Minds: How William James Can Save Your Life*, Kaag describes his approach as "a book that James might have written for men and women like Steven Rose [neuroscientist], a book that explores the 'maybe' of life's worth, and, for the time being, decides that it is worth enough."[73] Kaag argues that James's philosophy asserts that human genius is the faculty of perceiving in an unhabitual way, in an aesthetic manner.

Mihaly Csikszentmihalyi utilizes a cultural evolutionary point of view in likening creativity to the process of genetic changes that result in biological evolution:

> By random mutations, some individuals must have developed a nervous system in which the discovery of novelty stimulates the pleasure centers in the brain.

> Just as some individuals derive a keener pleasure from sex and others from food, so some must have been born who derived a keener pleasure from learning something new.[74]

Csikszentmihalyi's research looks at famous creative figures who are publicly successful and impactful, with an eye to better understand a way of being that is more satisfying than most lives typically are. He found that creativity results from the interaction of a system composed of three elements: a culture that contains symbolic rules, a person who brings novelty into the symbolic domain, and a field of experts who recognize and validate the innovation.

Csikszentmihalyi identifies seven elements in the social milieu that make creative contributions possible: training, expectations, resources, recognition, hope, opportunity, and reward. Complexity is the single most individual characteristic of creative people. Also, creative people take their hunches and own ideas more seriously than others.

Csikszentmihalyi coined the term *flow* to describe the state for artists (and others) when their abilities, work, and social context are in good alignment and therefore productive and personally fulfilling. He acknowledges that many activities productive of "flow" experiences have their origins in religious behaviors and that the values achieved in flow experiences have frequently been accorded a moral significance.[75]

Anton Ehrenzweig, an Austrian-born British theorist on modern art and modern music, wrote extensively about modern art from a psychological perspective. He argues that in many ways, creativity and mental illness are opposite sides of the same coin. The blocking of creativity could unleash the self-destructive fury of the superego, which in artistic practice is neutralized. For Ehrenzweig, creative work succeeds in coordinating the results of unconscious undifferentiation and conscious differentiation and reveals the hidden unconscious.

> Art is a dream dreamt by the artist which we, the wide awake spectators, can never see in its true structure; our waking faculties are bound to give us too precise an image produced by secondary revision.[76]

CONCLUSION

In this chapter, the history of Western aesthetics was reviewed, including the philosophical foundations, the role of religious groups, and notions of the sublime and transcendence. Also, the thoughts of modern and contemporary scholars were surveyed, along with contemporary perspectives on aesthetics. What are the patterns in the overwhelmingly rich and complex background to the field of aesthetics that is useful to consider when looking later at digital, biological, and everyday aesthetics?

Nietzsche's perspective on Greek drama points to the existential basis of art. Additionally, his thoughts about the pervasiveness of aesthetic experiences foreshadows the emerging field of everyday aesthetics discussed in Chapter 3.

Collingwood points to an artistic experience as the activity of consciousness. The emphasis moves from the art object to the perceiver in defining beauty. This shift is crucial to understanding the debate about consciousness and art when considering biological and computer art later in this book.

The close association of Christianity and art emphasizes the central role of art as culturally important. Furthermore, the notion of the sublime and transcendence through viewing and practicing the arts moves the focus from artists to an interaction with the natural physical world consistent with biological art detailed in the fifth chapter.

In contemporary aesthetics, the heated arguments about the death of art because of the interjection of philosophy into practice lays the groundwork for both digital and biological art. Questions about the role of human consciousness and the uniqueness of humans as creative organisms is at the center of the discussion at the end of the book.

In the next chapter, non-Western aesthetics are considered where several parallels to what has been presented here are found, as well as important divergences in thinking about art.

NOTES

1. Plato. (1941). *The republic of Plato*. Oxford, UK: Oxford University Press, p. 333.

2. Murdoch, I. (1999). *Existentialists and mystics: Writings on philosophy and literature*. New York: Penguin Books.

3. Aristotle. (1941). *The basic works of Aristotle*. New York: Random House, p. 1457.

4. Aristotle. (1941). *The basic works of Aristotle*. New York: Random House, p. 1450.

5. McDonald, M., & Walton, J.M. (2007). *The Cambridge companion to Greek and Roman theatre*. Cambridge, UK: Cambridge University Press.

6. Aristotle. (1941). *The basic works of Aristotle*. New York: Random House, p. 1450.

7. McDonald, M., & Walton, J.M. (2007). *The Cambridge companion to Greek and Roman theatre*. Cambridge, UK: Cambridge University Press ; Webster, T.B.L. (1970). *The Greek chorus*. London, UK: Methuen & Co.

8. Nietzsche, F. (1927). *The philosophy of Nietzsche.* New York: The Modern Library, p. 956.
9. Nietzsche, F. (1927). *The philosophy of Nietzsche.* New York: The Modern Library, p. 983.
10. Nietzsche, F. (1927). *The philosophy of Nietzsche.* New York: The Modern Library, p. 962–963.
11. Pollitt, J.J. (1972). *Art and experience in classical Greece.* Cambridge, UK: Cambridge University Press, p. 3.
12. Collingwood, R.G. (1938). *The principles of art.* Oxford, UK: Oxford at the Clarendon Press.
13. Herwitz, D. (2008). *Aesthetics: Key concepts in philosophy.* London, UK: Continuum International Publishing Group.
14. Collingwood, R.G. (1938). *The principles of art.* Oxford, UK: Oxford at the Clarendon Press, p. 118.
15. Collingwood, R.G. (1938). *The principles of art.* Oxford, UK: Oxford at the Clarendon Press, p. 274.
16. Mattes, M.C. (2017). *Martin Luther's theology of beauty: A reappraisal.* Grand Rapids, MI: Baker Academics ; Smith, P.H. (2004). *The body of the artisan: Art and experience in the scientific revolution.* Chicago, IL: The University of Chicago Press.
17. Spirituality and Christian Art. (2013). In Jones, T. D., Murray, L., & Murray, P. (Eds.), *The Oxford dictionary of Christian art and architecture.* Oxford, UK: Oxford University Press. Retrieved 30 Dec. 2021, from https://www-oxfordreference-com.ezproxy.lapl.org/view/10.1093/acref/9780199680276.001.0001/acref-9780199680276-e-1677.
18. Pslam 27:4
19. 13:5; cf. Rom. 1:20–23
20. Saliers, D.E. (2007). *Music and theology.* Nashville, TN: Abingdon Press.
21. Pattison, G. (1991). *Art, modernity and faith: Towards a theology of art.* New York: St. Martin's Press.
22. Exodus 20, v. 4.
23. Spirituality and Christian Art. (2013). In Jones, T. D, Murray, L., & Murray, P. (Eds.), *The Oxford dictionary of Christian art and architecture.* Oxford, UK: Oxford University Press. Retrieved 30 Dec. 2021, from https://www-oxfordreference-com.ezproxy.lapl.org/view/10.1093/acref/9780199680276.001.0001/acref-9780199680276-e-1677.
24. Dyrness, W.A. (2001). *Visual faith: Art, theology, and worship in dialogue.* Grand Rapids, MI: Baker Academic.
25. Mattes, M.C. (2017). *Martin Luther's theology of beauty: A reappraisal.* Grand Rapids, MI: Baker Academics.
26. Mattes, M.C. (2017). *Martin Luther's theology of beauty: A reappraisal.* Grand Rapids, MI: Baker Academics.
27. Smith, P.H. (2004). *The body of the artisan: Art and experience in the scientific revolution.* Chicago, IL: The University of Chicago Press.
28. Eco, U. (2002). *Art and beauty in the middle ages.* New Haven, CT: Yale University Press.

29. Eliade, M. (1990). *Symbolism, the sacred, and the arts.* New York: The Crossroad Publishing Company.

30. Mattes, M.C. (2017). *Martin Luther's theology of beauty: A reappraisal.* Grand Rapids, MI: Baker Academics.

31. Mattes, M.C. (2017). *Martin Luther's theology of beauty: A reappraisal.* Grand Rapids, MI: Baker Academics.

32. Elkins, J., & Morgan, D. (2009) *Re-enchantment.* New York: Routledge, p. 15.

33. Smith, P.H. (2004). *The body of the artisan: Art and experience in the scientific revolution.* Chicago, IL: The University of Chicago Press.

34. Mattes, M.C. (2017). *Martin Luther's theology of beauty: A reappraisal.* Grand Rapids, MI: Baker Academics.

35. Smith, P.H. (2004). *The body of the artisan: Art and experience in the scientific revolution.* Chicago, IL: The University of Chicago Press.

36. Bhattacharyya, A. (2020). From a context-bound to an essentializing conception: A study of Longinus's treatise on the sublime. *Journal of Comparative Literature and Aesthetics*, 43(2): 102–111. Retrieved from http://ezproxy.lapl.org/login?url=https://www.proquest.com/scholarly-journals/context-bound-essentializing-conception-study/docview/2465482262/se-2?accountid=6749

37. Begbie, J. (2018). *Redeeming transcendence in the arts: Bearing witness to the triune god.* Grand Rapids, MI: Eerdmans Publishing Co., p. 164.

38. Bowker, J. (2000). Mysticism. In *The concise Oxford dictionary of world religions.* Oxford University Press. Retrieved 30 December 2021, from https://www-oxfordreference-com.ezproxy.lapl.org/view/10.1093/acref/9780192800947.001.0001/acref-9780192800947-e-5021.

39. Alexander, S. R. (2021). "Oh my god!" exploring ecstatic experience through the evocative technology of gospel choir (Order No. 28772774). Available from ProQuest Central; Publicly Available Content Database. (2597477886). Retrieved from http://ezproxy.lapl.org/login?url=https://www.proquest.com/dissertations-theses/oh-my-god-exploring-ecstatic-experience-through/docview/2597477886/se-2

40. Newton, S.J. (2001). *Painting, psychoanalysis, and spirituality.* Cambridge, UK: Cambridge University Press.

41. Bychkov, V. (2021). The Russian symbolist Viacheslav Ivanov on aesthetic experience as religious. *Religions*, 12(2): 68. http://dx.doi.org/10.3390/rel12020068

42. Bychkov, V. (2021). The Russian symbolist Viacheslav Ivanov on aesthetic experience as religious. *Religions*, 12(2): 68. http://dx.doi.org/10.3390/rel12020068

43. Hodgkinson, V.A., & Weitzman, M.S. (1993). *From belief to commitment: The community service activities and finances of religious congregations in the United States.* Washington, DC: Independent Sector

44. Van Ness, P.H. (1996). *Spirituality and the secular quest.* New York: The Crossroad Publishing Company.

45. Wuthnow, R. (2001). *Creative spirituality: The way of the artist.* Berkeley, CA: University of California Press.

46. Lipsey, R. (1988). *An art of our own: The spiritual in twentieth century art.* Berkeley, CA: Shambhala Publications.

47. Brand, H., & Chaplin, A. (2001). *Art & soul: Signposts for Christians in the arts*. Carlisle, UK: Piquant, p. 16.

48. Appleton, H., & Nelstrop, L. (eds). (2018). *Art and mysticism: Interfaces in the medieval and modern periods*. New York: Routledge.

49. Manning, R.R. (2009). *The Cambridge companion to Paul Tillich*. Cambridge, UK: Cambridge University Press ; Van Ness, P.H. (1996). *Spirituality and the secular quest*. New York: The Crossroad Publishing Company.

50. Smith, P.H. (2004). *The body of the artisan: Art and experience in the scientific revolution*. Chicago, IL: The University of Chicago Press ; Fingesten, P. (1961) Spirituality, mysticism and non-Objective art. *Art Journal*, 21(1): 2–6, DOI: 10.1080/00043249.1961.10794175.

51. Brand, H., & Chaplin, A. (2001). *Art & soul: Signposts for Christians in the arts*. Carlisle, UK: Piquant, p. 15.

52. Elkins, J., & Morgan, D. (2009) *Re-enchantment*. New York: Routledge, p. 187.

53. Gablik, S. (1998). *The enchantment of art*. London, UK: Thames and Hudson, p. 42.

54. Díaz-Gilbert, M. (2018). The ascetic life of the ultrarunner. *Spiritus*, 18(2): 201–217. doi:http://dx.doi.org/10.1353/scs.2018.0025

55. Elkins, J., & Morgan, D. (2009) *Re-enchantment*. New York: Routledge, p. 216.

56. Danto, A.C. (1986). *Encounters & reflections: Art in the historical present*. New York: HarperCollins, p. 344.

57. Danto, A.C. (1986). *Encounters & reflections: Art in the historical present*. New York: HarperCollins, p. 334.

58. Haapala, A., Levinson, J., & Rantala, V. (1997). *The end of art and beyond: Essays after Danto*. Atlantic Highlands, NJ: Humanities Press International.

59. Haapala, A., Levinson, J., & Rantala, V. (1997). *The end of art and beyond: Essays after Danto*. Atlantic Highlands, NJ: Humanities Press International.

60. Danto, A. (1987). The art world. In Margolis, J. (ed). *Philosophy looks at the arts: Contemporary readings in aesthetics*. Philadelphia, PA: Temple University Press, p. 164.

61. Kuspit, D. (2004). *The end of art*. Cambridge, UK: Cambridge University Press, p. 69.

62. Kuspit, D. (2004). *The end of art*. Cambridge, UK: Cambridge University Press, p. 91.

63. Kuspit, D. (2004). *The end of art*. Cambridge, UK: Cambridge University Press, p. 127.

64. Carlson, A. (2009). *Nature & Landscape: An introduction to environmental aesthetics*. New York: Columbia University Press.

65. Carlson, A. (2009). *Nature & Landscape: An introduction to environmental aesthetics*. New York: Columbia University Press.

66. Murdoch, I. (1999). *Existentialists and mystics: Writings on philosophy and literature*. New York: Penguin Books.

67. Murdoch, I. (1999). *Existentialists and mystics: Writings on philosophy and literature*. New York: Penguin Books.

68. Johnson, R.A. (1989). *Ecstasy: Understanding the psychology of joy*. San Francisco, CA: HarperCollins.

69. Osmond, S. F. (1998, April). Art and the resurgent spiritual. *World and I*, 13(4), 100+. https://link.gale.com/apps/doc/A21185191/PPFA?u=lapl&sid=bookmark-PPFA&xid=9144c074

70. Kaag, J. (2020). *Sick souls, healthy minds: How William James can save your life*. Princeton, NJ: Princeton University Press, p. 180.

71. Kaag, J. (2020). *Sick souls, healthy minds: How William James can save your life*. Princeton, NJ: Princeton University Press, p. 115.

72. Kaag, J. (2020). *Sick souls, healthy minds: How William James can save your life*. Princeton, NJ: Princeton University Press, p. 155.

73. Kaag, J. (2020). *Sick souls, healthy minds: How William James can save your life*. Princeton, NJ: Princeton University Press, p. 9.

74. Csikszentmihalyi, M. (1996). *Creativity: Flow and the psychology of discovery and invention*. New York: HarperCollins, p. 109.

75. Van Ness, P.H. (1996). *Spirituality and the secular quest*. New York: The Crossroad Publishing Company.

76. Ehrenzweig, A. (1967). *The hidden order of art: A study in the psychology of artistic imagination*. Berkeley, CA: University of California Press, p. 79.

Chapter 2

Beyond Western Aesthetics

In this chapter, aesthetics outside Western culture is investigated with the intention of better understanding parallels and divergencies among civilizations and traditions. The influential philosopher George Santayana warns that art represents a paradox in human communication—in order to tell the truth about something so complicated, we need a conceptual apparatus that may conceal what it attempts to reveal.[1] Although inevitable bias comes from viewing one culture from another, this chapter intends specifically to delve into ideas and patterns further illuminating forward thinking in aesthetics.

The discussion starts with a brief consideration of anthropological perspectives on art. Artwork of various forms is a central part of studies of ancient civilizations, and scholars in the field are some of the major theoreticians about aesthetics. Those who research early human evidence of arts and artistic practice provide the starting point for understanding cross-cultural patterns and help us engage some of the common questions about the arts.

A brief survey of the extremely complex history of regional differences and influences follows. Four themes emerge from the analysis concentrating on disinterestedness, transcendence, process, and the pervasiveness of artistic activity.

ANTHROPOLOGICAL FOUNDATIONS

Why do humans make art? The arts exist in all human societies, as well as in predecessors of homo sapiens such as the Neanderthals. In music, different cultures typically utilize repetition and variation in their music, and employ rhythmic structures based on note length and dynamic stresses. Furthermore, scientists link music to natural selection—Darwin believed both sexes charmed each other with music and rhythm.[2]

However, there may be more to early art creation than simple reproductive urges. Ellen Dissanayake, in her book, *Art and Intimacy: How the Arts Began*, contends that the arts evolved not as stratagems for male competition, but as physical correlates of psychological concern.

> The biological phenomenon of love is originally manifested—expressed and exchanged—by means of emotionally meaningful "rhythms and modes" that are jointly created and sustained by mothers and their infants in ritualized, evolved interactions. From these rudimentary and unlikely beginnings grow adult expressions of love, both sexual and generally affiliative, and the arts. That is to say, in their origins in ourselves and in our species, love and art are, I suggest, inherently related.[3]

Dissanayake points to the problem for anthropologists making sense of the apparent early human desire to elaborate and decorate their primitive tools and other daily objects. Unlike other animals, humans characteristically do more than is necessary—they waste time lingering over their hands-on work. They transform the stuff of nature into culturally usable objects. This characteristic of "elaborating" is often overlooked by evolutionary biologists. What survival purpose is behind this elaborating?

According to Dissanayake, humans evolved to need participation in a group and find assurance that they could skillfully deal with the world. This psychological necessity was instilled and felt by means that are inherent in biological adaptation. She indicates that they appear in the hands-on making of objects.

> Unbound from their origins and elaborated as components of ceremony and, much later, as independent arts, rhythms and modes throughout most of human existence encapsulated and transmitted group meanings that further confirmed individual feelings of belonging, meaning, and competence and united individuals into like-minded, like-hearted groups.[4]

Art is an interactive behavior, hands-on, emotionally rewarding and psychologically meaningful, communal, and supportive of identity.

Finally, for Dissanayake, art is linked closely to religion and ritualistic practices. This is because the meaningful systems and stories by which religions explain the world and join their adherents in a common cause are everywhere expressed through art forms. Echoing Nietzsche, Dissanayake contends that rituals not only reinforce group belonging and meaning, but at the same time they are ways of addressing the uncertainty inherent in the human condition. Many ceremonies are motivated by anxiety and are structured so they deal with it in some way.

In general, the word *art* does not appear in nonliterate societies. In fact, even in Europe in the Middle Ages, very few objects were made exclusively to be contemplated. Art as a specific category is primarily limited to the

Figure 2.1. Celt with Incised Profile. Metropolitan Museum of Art, 10th–4th century BCE, Mexico, Mesoamerica, Olmec

Western tradition. What unites art in all societies is not its functional aspect, but rather its symbolic transformation of formal elements and stimulus of creativity. "Art makes the subconscious symbolic system real and objectively present."[5] Furthermore, art plays a key role in the maintenance of social groups in early societies.[6]

One strain of research in archaeology that arose in the early 1980s was a preoccupation with material culture as meaningful and symbolic. It explored ways some of the most abstract cultural practices are materially based.

> The history of human engagement with the material world is not so clearly one of mind being imposed on matter, or form on substance, but rather a history in which mind and matter, and form and substance continually bring each other into being.[7]

This material view of early human history views representational systems as drawing heavily upon the engaged adaptation with a physical world over millions of years.

Similarly, some scholars point to physical human response as a simple rationale for art:

> I propose that part of the emotional response to art results from reflexive reactions to certain configurations of line, shape, color, and sound, and that these reflexive emotional responses to certain visual and auditory images provide the rationale for the origin of art.[8]

In this way, specific lines, shapes, and colors evoke emotional responses in observers of art. This occurs not because of the observer's learned associations, but because of unconditioned human reflexes. These autonomic reactions are aesthetic responses.[9]

Stephen Davies, in *The Artful Species: Aesthetics, Art, and Evolution*, asks central questions about art and evolutionary biology. Are aesthetic behaviors the product of evolution because they directly helped humans survive and/or reproduce, or are they a by-product of evolutionary human behavior? Davies points out that the evolutionary biologists Stephen Jay Gould and Richard Lewontin introduce the term *spandrel* for evolutionary by-products with no functional significance of their own. The armpit is an example of a spandrel in the human body as it formed to join a limb to the body trunk and is a by-product. In this way, might art be a spandrel, an evolutionary by-product? Nevertheless, Davies notes that artistic behavior is a touchstone of humanity:

> They identify what is important to us as a species. They indicate what has directed our pathway and contributed to our success. Such behaviors are both puzzling and magnificent: puzzling because their inordinate cost seems to go

beyond what is necessary for survival, and magnificent because we take on their burden with such cheerful eagerness. They include our commitment to ritualized competition and to spirituality and religion. Among them, art behaviors are central. We are driven to be artists and art appreciators, as is testified by the place accorded to art in every society and epoch. Were we not so impelled, we would be less than fully human.[10]

A key topic to understand, in relationship to aesthetics and early humans, is the broader topic of human consciousness and ego. Thomas Metzinger, in his book *The Ego Tunnel: The Science of the Mind and the Myth of the Self*, argues there is no such thing as a self. "Contrary to what most people believe, nobody has ever been or had a self."[11] He contends that the appearance of worlds in biological nervous systems is a relatively recent phenomenon, perhaps only a few million years old.

In Darwinian evolution, an early form of consciousness might have arisen some two hundred million years ago in the primitive cerebral cortices of mammals, giving them bodily awareness and a sense of the surrounding world. The scientific evidence for the existence of such structures, not only in mammals, but also in birds and potentially in octopi, is strong. Metzinger notes that conscious experience is not an all-or-nothing phenomenon. This point is important to keep in mind when considering digital and biological art.

REGIONAL HISTORIES AND CONTRASTS

Most of the writing about non-Western art comes from the West and reflects 19th-century ideas about progress and social evolution. Former colonial powers often looked down on subjugated peoples as less sophisticated and artistic. "To people in Britain, France, Germany, and even the United States, the concept of art became associated with civilized refinement, beauty, and individual creative genius."[12]

Art studies in anthropology go back to the 19th-century beginnings of the discipline from Victorian scholars like Pitt-Rivers and Haddon in England, and Boas in America. Books including world art began to be published in the early 20th century typically as part of art history books. India, China, Japan, Korea, and other adjacent countries each encompass varying external influences, different conceptions of high and low art, and diverse aesthetic conceptions.[13]

After "primitive" art became a source for prominent avant-garde artists in Paris at the beginning of the 20th century, it was recognized as significant by some scholars and museums in New York during the 1930s and 1940s. By the 1970s, the reaction to the use of primitive terminology led to a variety of synonyms such as *tribal, ethnic, preindustrial, small scale,* and *preliterate*.[14]

It is useful to see how the field of world music in comparison to the visual arts has developed. One prominent scholar in the field defines current ethnomusicology as the study of music in culture from a comparative and egalitarian perspective. Principally, the field uses fieldwork for research to study musical manifestations of a society for the benefit of the world's musicians and the world's peoples.[15]

Comparative aesthetics as a discipline does not have the same long tradition as comparative philosophy or comparative religion. The beginning of writing about comparative aesthetics is marked by the notable 1934 book by Ananda Coomarswamy, *The Transformation of Nature in Art*. Afterward, articles in the *Journal of Aesthetics and Art Criticism* continued to develop the field. When Asian countries broke away from colonial rule, the field developed through formal conferences and exchanges. Translations of Sanskrit classics and Gnoli's book *The Aesthetic Experience According to Abhinavagupta* in 1956 were particularly important.[16]

Indian art was influenced by Greek art after the invasion by Alexander the Great, and then altered again by Saracen art after the Moslem invasion. For at least two centuries, India was considerably influenced by Western art.[17] Within India, aesthetics was typically not a separate area of study. However, there was intensive thinking about the basic principles of the various arts.

The Indian equivalent to the Western word "art" is *kala*. Anything made with a distinctive shape or form is considered a work of art, irrespective of fine arts or useful arts categorization. *Kala* has three distinct features: "It involves contemplative satisfaction both in creation and appreciation of art. It is a symbol which brings a concrete content directly before one's mind. It has a social function."[18]

Rasa is a distinguishing feature of Indian aesthetics, used metaphorically in literature to mean "juice" or "essence." It is the soul of art, and the pleasure it gives is transcendental. Yet art is not something divorced from the realities of life.

This is what is called *Rasa* in Indian aesthetics and beauty in European thought. The poet's art acts like a magic spell, makes the limitations of a person recede into the background and our blissful existence patent to us.[19]

Sanskrit drama evolved independently of other influences, then became affected greatly by ancient Greek theater. However, in general the type of drama found in Western tragedies doesn't make sense in India, where it is believed that there is ultimate happiness. The tragic form goes against the Indian sense of universal order and its philosophical temperament.[20]

In many cultures, music holds the highest position among the arts. H.I. Khan in *The Mysticism of Sound and Music: The Sufi Teaching of Hazrat*

Inayat Khan argues that music is the only art in which one can see "God free from all." Furthermore, he contends that life itself depends on rhythm and harmony: "Even all that we call matter or substance, and all that does not seem to speak or sound—it is all in reality vibration."[21] According to Khan, "This bliss of happiness and peace is available only to the Yogis and Sufis interested in the divine art of music."[22]

Japanese art was heavily influenced by Chinese culture but tends to view painting more as decoration, a less philosophical approach to painting. Conversely, the Chinese have a vast literature on the theory of painting.[23]

Another distinction between Chinese and Japanese art can be seen in landscape painting. The philosophical root of Chinese painting in Confucianism centers on a union with nature and careful technique.

In contrast, the Japanese Zen–inspired painter seeks the veracity of a landscape rather than concentrating on careful draftsmanship.

After long contemplation, he is expected to be able to seize inner truth in a swordlike stroke of the brush. . . . In their efforts to discover the very essence

Figure 2.2. *Reciting Poetry Before the Yellowing of Autumn.* LACMA, Wu Li (China, 1632–1718), Qing dynasty, 1674, Hanging scroll, ink on paper

of reality, the Zen artists turned away from the "emotional superficiality" of color and the "trivialities" of accurate detail. To them all natural phenomena were mere illusion, not to be copied painstakingly. They developed a highly stylized, seemingly spontaneous, black-and-white style to depict the various moods of nature and its inner reality.[24]

The brushstroke used in calligraphy is the basis of Eastern ink painting. The nature of Japanese writing as opposed to the Chinese also had its influence on the painting of the two peoples. The Japanese script tends to be smoother and far more cursive than the firm Chinese characters.[25]

By the late 19th century, Asian art exerted a strong influence on Western art. The first exhibition of Japanese art in London was held in 1854, and by the 1880s, appreciation of the Japanese color print especially found great popularity in Europe. In Japan the crafts were never scorned or considered inferior, and in fact many famous painters also worked as potters or as designers of lacquerware.[26]

Seyyed Hossein Nasr, in his comprehensive book *Islamic Art and Spirituality*, notes that the mathematical nature of Islamic art is in a sense the externalization of something hidden in the very structure of the Quran and the numerical symbolism of its letters and words. The Pythagorean philosophy of mathematics originating in Egypt and Babylon provided the language and presented an already elaborated science for Islam. The role of mathematics in the architecture in Islam is also important to understand: "Sacred architecture

Fig. 2.3. Banshō Zukan. Smithsonian Libraries, by Bunshichi Kobayashi

Figure 2.4. Designs from the Adina Mosque, Pandua, West Bengal. LACMA, India, West Bengal, Purroah (?), 1812, watercolors, Opaque watercolor and ink on paper

of Islam is a crystallization of Islamic spirituality and a key for the understanding of this spirituality."[27]

The mosque is the recapitulation of the harmony and order of mathematics. The striking domes are symbols of the heavenly vault. The void is central in Islamic architecture and explains the vast empty spaces in mosques.

The art of calligraphy reflects on the earthly plane the writing of Allah's word, as well as the intertwining of permanence and change. The world consists of a continuous flow of becoming, and Islamic calligraphy re-creates this metaphysical reality. Islamic patterns also often combine calligraphy with stylized forms or arabesques and geometric patterns.

Theater and music are limited in Islam in comparison to Western traditions. Since the Islamic religion is not based upon the dramatic tension between heaven and earth as in Western religions, a sacred and religious theater did not develop. Furthermore, there is a belief that one must be properly enlightened to listen to music.

> Islam has banned music which leads to the forgetfulness of God and has forbidden those Muslims from hearing it who would become distracted from the spiritual world and become immersed in worldliness through listening to music. But Islam has preserved from the whole community music in its most exalting and yet sober aspect. It has lent music a contemplative quality which is an echo of paradise and in which are combined the sensuous and the ascetic, the otherworldly and the beauty of the here and now.[28]

Perhaps as a result, literature takes on special importance in Islam, occupying a privileged position among the arts. Traditional poetry is innately logical, to the extent it is often used instead of a prosaic argument to prove a point. Rhythm is to be found at the heart of all incantatory spiritual practices based upon the traditional science of sounds, or mantra in Sanskrit.

Early writing about African art focuses on the impulse to copy natural forms and use them to convey meaning. Because humankind originated in Africa, some scholars suggest that perhaps art did as well. The problematic label of *tribal* or *primitive* art has had a negative impact on the field of African art and meant that until recently little academic interest was shown in regional differences or individual artists.[29]

In keeping with regressive social evolutionary theories, social scientists in the past identified African art as "primeval." Textbooks of the early 20th century presented all African arts as conceptually like prehistoric works or to the arts of children. Nevertheless, a great deal of African art has a religious purpose.[30] Much of African art is in the form of handmade sculptures. Something made by hand, or *alonuzo*, is how the Fon of Benin designate art. The nearby Ewe of Togo use a similar term, *adanu*, meaning skill and value, to refer at once to art and ornamentation.

The earliest sculptural tradition outside of Egypt is found in Nigeria. The human figure is the most frequent sculptural motif. Such works have often been referred to as ancestor figures, yet the degree to which they represent specific historical forebears is unclear. It may be that sculptures were originally created to represent shrine owners.[31]

CROSS-CULTURAL PATTERNS

In addition to discussing specific cultural and historical traditions, it is useful to analyze world art in terms of consistent themes. This approach allows us to see how trends inform contemporary biological, digital, and everyday aesthetics.

While there are certainly many cross-cultural aesthetic parallels, there are also very pointed differences linked to cultural history, and especially religious beliefs. While one dominant strain of Western aesthetics is consumed with defining the specific characteristics of great art and artists, many non-Western traditions concentrate instead on transcendence, process, and the pervasiveness of beauty.

Beauty in Disinterestedness

Western society in many ways is built on the celebration of the individual human ego, while much of Eastern philosophy strives for selflessness, particularly in artistic expression and appreciation. Nevertheless, there are some parallels in thinking. For instance, Immanuel Kant's aesthetic disinterest is like the Japanese notion of beauty as artistic detachment seen in traditional Zen aestheticism and in the Kyoto school of modern Japanese philosophy.[32]

It is important to clarify what Kant and other Western philosophers mean by "disinterest." It does not mean uninterested, but rather a state devoid of self-interest. Disinterest is opposed to self-interest. In fact, the notion of disinterestedness can be traced from one German philosopher to another. Schiller made Kant's idea of disinterested appreciation of beauty a key element in the process of aesthetic education. Schopenhauer elevated the Kantian notion of disinterestedness into an act of Buddhistic *nirvana*. Nietzsche then attacked aesthetic disinterestedness, arguing instead for the Dionysian concept of beauty as rapture or ecstasy. Heidegger in the 20th century defended Kant's theory of aesthetic disinterestedness with his notion of letting-be, an attitude of openness to beauty.[33]

The Indian *rasa* theory, discussed earlier, is one of the earliest world theories of artistic detachment. In Abhinavagupta's theory of "peaceful beauty," a doctrine of artistic detachment is explicitly formulated. Aesthetic detachment of *rasa* is considered supreme bliss.[34]

Japanese *wabi sabi* art is built on the precepts of simplicity, naturalness, melancholy, and impermanence. If an object or expression elicits a sense of melancholy and spiritual longing, then it is *wabi sabi*. According to *wabi sabi* thinking, the idea that we are separate from the outside world and objects is illusionary. "In modern psychological terms, a child becomes ego-centric when he has learned to distinguish himself from the world he perceives. It is just this learned idea that we are separate from our environment that Zen says we need to unlearn."[35] In reframing the self-conception, real art and creativity can occur.

D. T. Suzuki, in his influential *Zen and Japanese Culture*, describes Zen as one of the products of the Chinese mind after its contact with Indian thought, introduced into China in the 1st century AD through the medium of Buddhist teachings. The aesthetic aspect of Zen teaching is closely related to the absence of selfhood and the merging of subject and object in one absolute emptiness, or *sunyata*.[36]

According to Suzuki, the artist's world is one of free creation, unhampered by senses and intellect. The "one-corner" style of Japanese art is associated with the technique of using the least possible number of lines or strokes to represent forms on silk or paper. For instance: "A simple fishing boat in the midst of the rippling waters is enough to awaken in the mind of the beholder a sense of the vastness of the sea and at the same time of peace and contentment—the Zen sense of the Alone."[37]

Furthermore, Suzuki notes that in the Zen tradition, beauty is not necessarily linked to perfection of form. "This has been one of the favorite tricks of Japanese artists—to embody beauty in a form of imperfection or even of ugliness."[38] The Japanese Zen tradition focuses specifically on the aesthetic experience of beauty manifested by ordinary phenomena: "What is distinctive about Zen aestheticism is its emphasis on enlightenment through detached contemplation of beauty in nature and art."[39]

Figure 2.5. Japanese Landscape. Landscape traditionally attributed to Sesshū Tōyō, Muromachi period, 15th century, ink on paper, Honolulu Museum of Art accession 2846

At the core of D. T. Suzuki's treatment of Japanese aesthetics is the Zen doctrine of *mushin*, or "no-mind." Zen ideals of beauty, which include mystery, rustic poverty, loneliness, and windblown elegance, are all to be analyzed as a function of ego-lessness, or *mushin*. Finally, the supreme moment in the life of a Zen artist is the experience of *satori*, becoming conscious of the unconscious.

Many scholars in different fields within the arts contrast the Western focus on the individual and human ego to the Eastern tendency to embrace the collective or group. Jacques Maritain, in his book *Creative Intuition in Art and Poetry*, distinguishes Asian from Western art's focus on the human anatomy:

> Chinese art, however, despite its interest in portraiture, has not yet perceived the privileged beauty of the human figure. It is less interested in the beauty of the human body than in the beauty of landscapes, birds, and flowers. Some of the traits I just pointed out make Chinese art, in one sense, nearer than Indian art to our own art. It remains, nevertheless, dominated by the supremacy of Things over the human Self which characterizes Oriental art in general.[40]

According to Maritain, Asian art opposes Western individualism in that it endeavors to hide the human self and to concentrate on the physical world. It is primarily directed toward communion with the sacred natural world. Maritain describes the relationship between nature and man in Eastern thinking as a kind of "interpenetration." Each of the two remains what it is, while it experiences the fertilization of the other. "They are mysteriously commingled."[41]

In the Indian tradition:

> The artist is not a special kind of man, but every man who is not an artist in some field, every man without a vocation, is an idler. The kind of artist that a man should be, carpenter, painter, lawyer, farmer or priest, is determined by his own nature, in other words by his nativity.[42]

Beauty of Spirituality and Transcendence

The deeply intertwined history of Western aesthetics with Judeo-Christian traditions is evident. In non-Western traditions, the same linkage of attitudes regarding art to religious and philosophical movements is clear.

Sanskrit literary theory attaches profound importance to the function of spiritual suggestion because through it is reached the profound bliss of the infinite. In fact, all real poetry must give a hint of the infinite, serving "as the bridge between the Small and the Sublime, the Finite and Infinite."[43] Universalization, technically known as *sadharanikarana* in the terminology, is the process through which one becomes free from the limitations of the individual ego. "As the appreciator experiences a strong sense of Wonder his mind receives a violent concussion and consequently the flow of thoughts concerning his ordinary joy and sorrow—hope and despair—gain and loss is suspended for the time being."[44]

Art and religion are complementary responses to the quest for self-realization. While religion encourages one to become like a child, art urges artists to return to primordial innocence. Religious artworks are intermediaries in the process:

> Art, like nature, can serve as a vehicle by which humans reach for the divine. I further contend that humans, who are aesthetic as well as rational beings, cannot fully encounter God without song, however simple, or without poetry, however elementary.[45]

The most fundamental common denominator between art and religion is the quest for unity or oneness. One scholar claims there are three types of unity: self-integration, in an object of attention, and union with others. Great art and religion are allied practices because they are both attempts to promote harmony within the self or between the self and the divine. "Because humans long for wholeness, art and religion are most satisfying when they reconcile tensions, calm and dissipate fears, mitigate sorrows, or wring unity out of opposites."[46]

One Japanese artist writes passionately about the relationship between artistic practice and spirituality:

> I now consider what I do in the studio to be theological work as much as aesthetic work. I experience God my Maker, in the studio. I am immersed in the art of creating, and I have come to understand this dimension of life as the most profound way of grasping human experience and the nature of our existence in the world. I call it the "Theology of Making."[47]

Thomas R. Martland, in *Religion as Art: An Interpretation*, argues that art and religion present collectively created frames of perception and meaning by which people interpret their experiences and order their lives. "Art and religion provide the patterns of meaning, the frames of perception, by which society interprets its experiences and from which it makes conclusions about the nature of its world."[48]

Martland views *innocence* as an appropriate term for describing the attitude of those who are engaged in artistic and religious activity. The artist and religious person willingly detach themselves from current understandings, either by sacrificing the ego construct through which they understand the world or by suspending judgment. The artist willingly creates or finds new understandings by incorporating experiences previously ignored. "What they all lack—the magician, the craftsman, and the inventor—is freedom from the urge to control, willingness to let go of their expectations, and willingness to absorb whatever discoveries may come."[49]

Some regard dance as movement meditation, another kind of prayer. The body is another way of working with the psychic force in the universe. According to Eastern thought, dance is a primordial art. American Ruth St. Denis, a primary force in the teaching of dance in America, wrote about the universality of dance:

> In its deepest sense, all movement in rhythm is religious, revealing in the body the cosmic eternal rhythms of the university. The Hindus long ago set up the symbol of Shiva as the Lord of the cosmic dance because they knew that everything in the universe dances its way into manifestation.[50]

For artists working with their hands, and dancers especially, spiritual knowledge can come through the body.

> If you cannot honor your body and learn from the body's wisdom, it seems to me something is missing in your spirituality. We are incarnate. It is the central part of Christianity, incarnation, resurrection. It's a schizophrenic split if people cannot connect that with the body.[51]

An emphasis on mystery is something artists talk about and express continually in their art.

> I see my work as research and the research is into the unknown. What is the next painting going to look like? What is that feeling and that mood inside me? What am I thinking that I can't think out loud? What is it going to look like? That sense of the adventure, the imagination, the wonder of creating something. My work is about mystery. My work is not about revealing the mystery, but saying that "Mystery is present here." Notice it![52]

According to Earle J. Coleman, transcendence is a common denominator of aesthetic and spiritual states. To realize what is true eternally, artists and mystics need to transcend time and space. Additionally, an attitude of receptivity is another shared feature of the aesthetic and the spiritual. Usually, this state of acceptance precedes the mystic's illumination and the artist's inspiration or afflation. Coleman quotes an appropriate Navajo prayer:

> With beauty before me, I walk
> With beauty behind me, I walk
> With beauty above me, I walk
> With beauty below me, I walk
> From the East beauty has been restored

Figure 2.6. *Shiva as the Lord of Dance.* LACMA, India, Madhya Pradesh, circa 800, Sculpture, Red sandstone

> From the South beauty has been restored
> From the West beauty has been restored
> From the zenith in the sky beauty has been restored
> From the nadir of the earth beauty has been restored
> From all around me beauty has been restored.[53]

Similarly, Coleman points to Walt Whitman's transcendent poetry: "To me every hour of the dark and light is a miracle/Every cubic inch of space is a miracle."

When contemporary artists embark on a spiritual journey, it is typically one into the unknown, often at great cost to them in practical terms.

> Many of us, whether we are aware of it or not, look to visual artists, writers, and musicians for spiritual guidance, insight, and inspiration. Artists are sometimes among the few who take time to reflect on the deeper meaning of life and to search for ways to express both the turmoil of their search and the tentative insights they have gained. They usually have more questions than answers, yet their work celebrates wholeness and coherence as well as bewilderment and mystery.[54]

Artists are in some ways religious practitioners. Few have received conventional religious training, but their work stirs the soul, reflects engagement with religious traditions, and raises profound questions.

Beauty of Imperfection and Process

In contrast to Western customs, Eastern aesthetics suggests that ordered structures in art are contrived. Soetsu Yanagi, in *The Beauty of Everyday Things*, contends that the Western perception of art is rooted in ancient Greece and its obsession with perfectionism consistent with rational tendencies. It is the "art of even numbers."

In contrast to this, what the Japanese eye seeks is the beauty of imperfection, which Yanagi terms the "art of odd numbers." No other country pursues the art of imperfection as eagerly as Japan. For example, in painting, the term *Zuihitsu* implies following the brush, allowing the tool to lead. Many Japanese writers also prize a quality of vacillation in the structure of their work.[55]

Creating beautiful objects in this model should be free and unrestrained, as easy and thoughtless as walking. Looking at specific Japanese arts, Yanagi argues that patterns represent what is most clearly seen in nature, that they condense what we see in the natural world. Compared to nature in the raw or representational landscapes, patterned nature is infinitely more beautiful. Through good patterns we see the secrets of beauty.[56]

Figure 2.7. *Evening Rain at Karasaki.* Library of Congress, Katsushika, Hokusai, 1760–1849, artist

Chinese artists also deemphasize composition within the frame. Instead, fragments are stressed, representative of eternity.

What the Chinese artist records is not a single visual confrontation, but an accumulation of experience touched off perhaps by one moment's exaltation before the beauty of nature. The experience is transmitted in forms that are not merely generalized, but also richly symbolic."[57]

Chinese artists deny the concept of completion of an art piece. The Chinese painter avoids any claim of completion as a presumption beyond the power of an artist. "All he can do is to liberate the imagination and set it wandering over the limitless spaces of the universe. His landscape is not a final statement, but a starting point; not an end, but the opening of a door."[58]

Beauty Every Day

In non-Western civilizations, there is typically much less of a division between the arts and daily life. Some cultures pursue a lifestyle consciously built on aesthetic customs and practices meant to celebrate ubiquitous beauty.

One can see aesthetic principles revealed in the elaborate tea-drinking practices found in Asia. Tea ceremonies originated in China, where it was popular among the monks and then was introduced into Japan through the Zen sect. There it was refined and subsequently influenced pottery design and other arts, such as architecture and painting. Swann describes the difference between the practices in China and Japan:

> In China a recluse, perhaps with a few friends, would drink his tea before some broad landscape and contemplate a famed panorama; in Japan everything was reduced in scale and the grandeur of nature was simulated by the most cunning landscape gardening. Peace, respect, rustic serenity, and solitude were the aims of the ceremony in its purest form.[59]

According to one scholar, "The tearoom is to *wabi sabi* what the church is to Christianity."[60] Tea service became an art in which the host and guests celebrated the mundane, physical world.

In Japan, cast-iron kettles as objects of art developed from the tea ceremony and lifted them out of the common kitchen into what became the cultivated "rustic style." In this influential movement, the humbler an object, the more beautiful.[61] The characteristics of *wabi sabi* as an art involve no shiny, uniform materials, but instead ones that show the passage of time. The form comes from the physical properties of the materials used, in a natural and unforced way. Subdued lighting and colors from natural sources are often used.

During the long years of its seclusion, Japan became so internalized that aesthetics took the place accorded religion in other countries. Japanese

Figure 2.8. *Tea Ceremony Apparatus*. Metropolitan Museum of Art, Shibata Zeshin (Japanese, 1807–1891), Edo period

culture became structured with its aesthetic values at the center. Art is practiced as a way of life. "Mono no aware" is a person's ability to realize the moving power of external reality.[62]

Beyond Western Aesthetics 57

Figure 2.9. Cold-water Container for Tea. LACMA, Japan, Momoyama period, 1573–1615; circa 1615, Ceramics Shigaraki ware, stoneware, naturally occurring ash glaze, lacquer

Folk craft objects have two principal features: they are things made for daily use and are commonly found. Through raising the ordinary things of our daily lives to a higher level, an unconscious graceful life is created.

Craftspeople are said to practice a blessed unawareness.[63] This Japanese conception of art links very closely to contemporary everyday aesthetics, presented in the next chapter. According to Suzuki, Zen is a religion of beauty wherein aesthetic and spiritual values are identical. "Hence the ultimate goal of Zen aestheticism is not the creation of external artworks such as ink wash painting, poetry, or drama but the creative transformation of one's own everyday life into a work of art."[64]

Consistent with some other non-Western cultures, art from Indian traditions does not make a distinction between fine art and craft, or folk, art.

> Primitive man, despite the pressure of his struggle for existence, knew nothing of such merely functional arts. The whole man is naturally a metaphysician, and only later on a philosopher and psychologist, a systematist. His reasoning is by analogy, or in other words by means of an "adequate symbolism." As a person rather than an animal he knows immortal through mortal things.[65]

In this way, works of art dynamically mix the utilitarian and the spiritual, the physical and metaphysical. Paralleling everyday aesthetics, every person is an artist in some sense. Artistic works are unearthed rather than invented by a unique talent.

> No man, considered as so-and-so, can be a genius: but all men have a genius, to be served or disobeyed at their own peril. There can be no property in ideas, because these are gifts of the Spirit and not to be confused with talents: ideas are never made, but can only be "invented," that is "found," and entertained.[66]

For this reason, art pieces are typically not signed in Indian culture. In traditional oriental art, the focus is on the content rather than the artist.

In the Navajo world, art is similarly unseparated from everyday life. Indeed, nearly all Navajos are artists and spend a large part of their time in artistic creation. The creation of beauty and the incorporation of oneself in beauty represent the highest attainment and ultimate destiny of man. Art is not an abstractable quality; it is the normal pattern in nature and the most desirable form of experience.

For the Navajo, beauty is not so much in the eye of the beholder as it is in the mind of its creator and the relationship to the art object. The Navajo does not look for beauty; he generates it within himself and projects it onto the universe.[67]

Thinking and singing the world into existence attributes a definite kind of power to thought and song to which most Westerners are not accustomed. In the Navajo view of the world, language is not a mirror of reality; reality is a mirror of language. Symbols have concrete reality for them. Both substance and symbol are primordial. So-called Holy People are seen as representing the spiritual world in Navajo culture, and the main relationship is then between Holy People and the people of the earth.

The Holy People of the Fifth World are the inner forms of various natural phenomena and forces, including animals, and are the controlling and animating powers of nature. Beauty is an essential condition of man's life and is dynamic. It is not in things so much as it is in the dynamic relationships among things and between man and things: "Man experiences beauty by creating it." Navajo culture advocates an artistic way of life: "One is admonished to walk in beauty, speak in beauty, act in beauty, sing in beauty, and live in beauty. All things are to be made beautifully, and all activities are to be completed in beauty."[68]

Eskimos have no equivalent to the words *create* or *make*. The closest Eskimo term means "to work on," which also involves an act of will, but one that is restrained. The Eskimo carver never attempts to force ivory or wood into uncharacteristic forms but instead responds to the material as it tries to be itself, and thus the carving is continually modified.

> Carvers make no effort to develop personal styles and take no care to be remembered as individuals, but simply disappear, as it were, behind their works. Their goal is not to develop unique art styles, not to present personal views, nor even to bring to fruition biases peculiar to them personally; rather, it is to express to

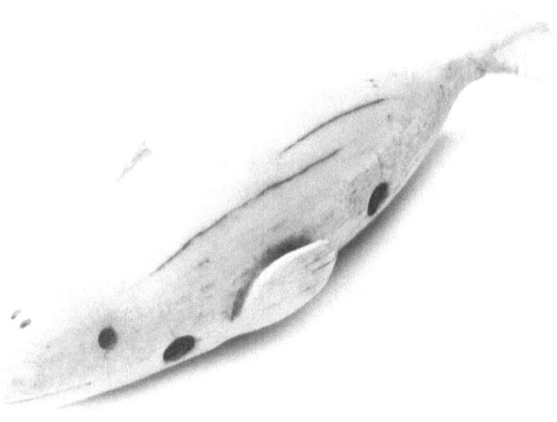

Figure 2.10. Eskimo Carving. Source: LACMA, United States, Alaska, Native American, Eskimo, early 19th century

perfection a timeless tradition, breathing into it "the breath of life" so that each form is fresh, though the grammar is never violated.[69]

The Eskimo artist is said to emphasize "all-at-onceness"—mythic forms that illuminate all levels at the same time.

CONCLUSION

This chapter delved into the complex comparative aesthetics found outside Western culture. Those scholars studying early humans note the common artistic urge appears and how integrated it has been in daily life. Craft, tools, and art in many cases are indistinguishable. Both Western and non-Western art are profoundly linked to formal religions, spiritual longing, and existential questioning.

> Great art has been connected to every great spiritual tradition because art is always a crystallized devotion to a world in process. The deepest spiritual experiences of many peoples have been, or have entwined with, the making and using of works of art, or with engagement in absorbing process.[70]

Mental preparation for an aesthetic encounter is like meditation in some classical Eastern traditions. Concentrating one's attention on the visible object is the first condition for aesthetic perception, as in Yoga Sutra's mental discipline. If aesthetic vision is a manifestation of contemplation, we may conclude the aesthetic perception is culturally universal.[71]

Important themes emerged in this chapter that directly and indirectly inform contemporary theories about everyday aesthetics, including notions of process and the pervasiveness of creative practice. Non-Western art in particular sets the stage for the exploration of everyday aesthetics, the subject of the next chapter, and for the presentation of contemporary digital and biological art in the fourth and fifth chapters.

NOTES

1. Sprigge, T.L.S. (1974). *Santayana: An examination of his philosophy*. London, UK: Routledge.

2. Mithen, S. (2006). *The singing Neanderthals*. Cambridge, MA: Harvard University Press.

3. Dissanayake, E. (2000). *Art and intimacy: How the arts began*. Seattle, WA: University of Washington Press, p. xi.

4. Dissanayake, E. (2000). *Art and intimacy: How the arts began*. Seattle, WA: University of Washington Press, p. 168.

5. Alland, A. (1977). *The artistic animal: An inquiry into the biological roots of art*. Garden City, NY: Anchor Books, p. 20.

6. Maquet, J. (1986). *The aesthetic experience: An anthropologist looks at the visual arts*. New Haven, CT: Yale University Press.

7. Boivin, N. (2008). *Material cultures, material minds: The impact of things on human thought, society, and evolution*. Cambridge, UK: Cambridge University Press, p. 23.

8. Aiken, N.E. (1998). *The biological origins of art*. Westport, CT: Praeger, p. 3.

9. Aiken, N.E. (1998). *The biological origins of art*. Westport, CT: Praeger.

10. Davies, S. (2012). *The artful species: Aesthetics, art, and evolution*. Oxford, UK: Oxford University Press, p. 188.

11. Metzinger, T. (2010). The ego tunnel: The science of the mind and the myth of the self. New York: Basic Books, p. 1.

12. Venbrux, E., Rosi, P.S., & Welsch, R.L. (2006). *Exploring world art*. Long Grove, IL: Waveland Press, Inc., p. 2.

13. Zijlmans, K., & Van Damme, W. (2008). *World art studies: Exploring concepts and approaches*. Amsterdam: Valiz..

14. Venbrux, E., Rosi, P.S., & Welsch, R.L. (2006). *Exploring world art*. Long Grove, IL: Waveland Press, Inc.

15. Nettl, B. (2015). *The study of ethnomusicology: Thirty-three discussions*. Urbana, IL: University of Illinois Press.

16. Chaudhary, A. (1991). *Comparative aesthetics: East and West*. Delhi, India: Eastern Book Linkers.

17. Rao, G.H. (1974). *Comparative aesthetics: Eastern and Western*. India: Mysore Printing and Publishing House.

18. Rao, G.H. (1974). *Comparative aesthetics: Eastern and Western*. India: Mysore Printing and Publishing House, p. 195.

19. Chaudhary, A. (1991). *Comparative aesthetics: East and West*. Delhi, India: Eastern Book Linkers, p. 52.

20. Chaudhary, A. (1991). *Comparative aesthetics: East and West*. Delhi, India: Eastern Book Linkers.

21. Khan, H.I. (1996). *The mysticism of sound and music: The Sufi teaching of Hazrat Inayat Khan*. Boston, MA: Shambhala Dragon Editions, p. 18.

22. Khan, H.I. (1996). *The mysticism of sound and music: The Sufi teaching of Hazrat Inayat Khan*. Boston, MA: Shambhala Dragon Editions, p. 10.

23. Swann, P.C. (1958). *A concise history of Japanese art*. Tokyo, Japan: Kodansha International Ltd.

24. Swann, P.C. (1958). *A concise history of Japanese art*. Tokyo, Japan: Kodansha International Ltd., p. 178.

25. Swann, P.C. (1958). *A concise history of Japanese art*. Tokyo, Japan: Kodansha International Ltd.

26. Swann, P.C. (1958). *A concise history of Japanese art*. Tokyo, Japan: Kodansha International Ltd.

27. Nasr, S.H. (1987). *Islamic art and spirituality*. Albany, NY: State University of New York Press, p. 59.
28. Nasr, S.H. (1987). *Islamic art and spirituality*. Albany, NY: State University of New York Press, p. 160.
29. Willett, F. (2002). *African art*. London. New York: Thames & Hudson ; Visona, M.B., Poynor, R., Cole, H.M., & Harris, M.D. (2001). *A history of art in Africa*. London, UK: Harry N. Abrams, Inc., Publishers.
30. Willett, F. (2002). *African art*. London. New York: Thames & Hudson.
31. Visona, M.B., Poynor, R., Cole, H.M., & Harris, M.D. (2001). *A history of art in Africa*. London, UK: Harry N. Abrams, Inc., Publishers.
32. Odin, S. (2001). *Artistic detachment in Japan and the West: Psychic distance in comparative aesthetics*. Honolulu, HI: University of Hawaii Press.
33. Odin, S. (2001). *Artistic detachment in Japan and the West: Psychic distance in comparative aesthetics*. Honolulu, HI: University of Hawaii Press.
34. Odin, S. (2001). *Artistic detachment in Japan and the West: Psychic distance in comparative aesthetics*. Honolulu, HI: University of Hawaii Press.
35. Juniper, A. (2003). Wabi Sabi: The Japanese art of impermanence. Tokyo, Japan: Tuttle Publishing, p. 24.
36. Suzuki, D.T. (1973). *Zen and Japanese culture*. Princeton, NJ: Princeton University Press.
37. Suzuki, D.T. (1973). *Zen and Japanese culture*. Princeton, NJ: Princeton University Press, p. 22.
38. Suzuki, D.T. (1973). *Zen and Japanese culture*. Princeton, NJ: Princeton University Press, p. 24.
39. Odin, S. (2001). *Artistic detachment in Japan and the West: Psychic distance in comparative aesthetics*. Honolulu, HI: University of Hawaii Press, p. 100.
40. Maritain, J. (1953). *Creative intuition in art and poetry*. New York: Pantheon Books, p. 17.
41. Maritain, J. (1953). *Creative intuition in art and poetry*. New York: Pantheon Books, p. 19.
42. Coomaraswamy, A.K. (1956). *Christian and oriental philosophy of art*. New York: Dover Publications Inc., p. 24.
43. Mukherji, R. (1991). *Comparative aesthetics: Indian and Western*. Calcutta, India: Sanskrit Pustak Bhandar, p. 14.
44. Mukherji, R. (1991). *Comparative aesthetics: Indian and Western*. Calcutta, India: Sanskrit Pustak Bhandar, p. 45.
45. Coleman, E.J. (1998). *Creativity and spirituality: Bonds between art and religion*. Albany, NY: State University of New York Press, p. xvii.
46. Coleman, E.J. (1998). *Creativity and spirituality: Bonds between art and religion*. Albany, NY: State University of New York Press, p. xviii–xix.
47. Fujimura, M. (2020). *Art and faith: A theology of making*. New Haven, CT: Yale University Press, p. 3.
48. Martland, T.R. (1981). *Religion as art: An interpretation*. Albany, NY: New York State University Press, p. 12.

49. Martland, T.R. (1981). *Religion as art: An interpretation.* Albany, NY: New York State University Press, p. 86.

50. Miller, K.A. (1997). *Wisdom comes dancing: Selected writings of Ruth St. Denis on dance, spirituality, and the body.* Seattle, WA: Peace Works, p. 73.

51. Wuthnow, R. (2001). *Creative spirituality: The way of the artist.* Berkeley, CA: University of California Press, p. 180.

52. Wuthnow, R. (2001). *Creative spirituality: The way of the artist.* Berkeley, CA: University of California Press, p. 32.

53. Coleman, E.J. (1998). *Creativity and spirituality: Bonds between art and religion.* Albany, NY: State University of New York Press, p. 61.

54. Wuthnow, R. (2001). *Creative spirituality: The way of the artist.* Berkeley, CA: University of California Press, p. 266–67.

55. Yanagi, S. (2019). *The beauty of everyday things.* New York: Penguin Modern Classics.

56. Yanagi, S. (2019). *The beauty of everyday things.* New York: Penguin Modern Classics.

57. Sullivan, M. (1967). *A short history of Chinese art.* Berkeley, CA: University of California Press, p. 182.

58. Sullivan, M. (1967). *A short history of Chinese art.* Berkeley, CA: University of California Press, p. 183.

59. Swann, P. C. (1958). *A concise history of Japanese art.* Tokyo, Japan: Kodansha International Ltd., p. 7.

60. Juniper, A. (2003). *Wabi Sabi: The Japanese art of impermanence.* Tokyo, Japan: Tuttle Publishing, p. 32.

61. Swann, P.C. (1958). *A concise history of Japanese art.* Tokyo, Japan: Kodansha International Ltd.

62. Marra, M.F. (2001). *A history of modern Japanese aesthetics.* Oahu, HI: University of Hawaii Press.

63. Yanagi, S. (2019). *The beauty of everyday things.* New York: Penguin Modern Classics.

64. Odin, S. (2001). *Artistic detachment in Japan and the West: Psychic distance in comparative aesthetics.* Honolulu, HI: University of Hawaii Press, p. 148.

65. Coomaraswamy, A.K. (1956). *Christian and oriental philosophy of art.* New York: Dover Publications Inc., p. 31.

66. Coomaraswamy, A.K. (1956). *Christian and oriental philosophy of art.* New York: Dover Publications Inc., p. 38.

67. Witherspoon, G. (1977). *Language and art in the Navajo universe.* Ann Arbor, MI: University of Michigan Press.

68. Witherspoon, G. (1977). *Language and art in the Navajo universe.* Ann Arbor, MI: University of Michigan Press, p. 152.

69. Carpenter, E. Image making in artic art. In Kepes, G. (ed.) (1966), *Sign image symbol.* New York: George Braziller, p. 214.

70. Sartwell, C. (1995). *The art of living: Aesthetics of the ordinary in world spiritual traditions*. Albany, NY: State University of New York Press, p. xiii.

71. Maquet, J. (1986). *The aesthetic experience: An anthropologist looks at the visual arts*. New Haven, CT: Yale University Press.

Chapter 3

The Aesthetics of the Everyday

The aesthetics of the everyday is a relatively recent development originating in 18th- and 19th-century European and American philosophy and informed especially by non-Western thinking. The roots of this emerging philosophy come from the appreciation of beauty in nature, as especially seen in European romanticism. In America, Ralph Waldo Emerson and the transcendentalists were a crucial influence on John Dewey, who wrote *Art as Experience*, the key text for the thought movement. Dewey's democratization of art makes creative work potentially more accessible to all.

In this chapter, questions posed at the beginning about the nature of human engagement with beauty on a fundamental basis are directly addressed. The contentions and evolving new directions of the aesthetics of the everyday are explored, as well as linkages to digital and biological art forms.

EUROPEAN PRECURSORS

Among the first Westerners to attempt a scientific look at the nature of beauty was William Hogarth, who in 1752 published an article on "The Analysis of Beauty," inviting readers to pick the most beautiful of a series of images (corsets, noses, haircuts, table legs), concluding that the right choice involved proper curves. He also asserted a psychological principle that centuries later influenced machines making art—that humans love variety, but not too much.[1] Armstrong, in his book *The Secret Power of Beauty*, elaborates on Hogarth's important theory about art appreciation and variety:

> The most pleasing things are those that simultaneously reward our desire for variety and respect our need for uniformity—perfectly balancing stimulation and repose, excitement and security. The experience of beauty is the mid-point between boredom and exhaustion.[2]

While Hogarth's experiments leave much to be desired in modern terms, his general notion about the viewer wanting consistency with small variation continues to contemporary times (as seen in the formal programming of learning machines discussed in the next chapter).

A new period in the relationship between religion and art was brought about by the rise of romanticism at the end of the 18th century. Romanticism is a loose philosophical and literary movement that is identified with specific groups in Germany, England, and America. The "Jena Set" in Germany may be the most influential of the groups and was first to use the term *romantic*.

The Jena Set involved Goethe, Schiller, Schelling, Novalis, Fichte, Humboldt, and Karl and Caroline Schlegel. They heavily impacted the other groups, who shared similar ideas such as the British romantic poets (Coleridge, Wordsworth, Blake, Byron, Shelley, Keats), the North American transcendentalists (Emerson, Thoreau, Hawthorne), and the later Bloomsbury group (Woolf, Forster, Bell, Keynes).

In their day, the members of the Jena cluster were so famous that their movements and thoughts were discussed throughout the world.[3]

> They were talking about the bond between art and life, between the individual and society, between humankind and nature. Just as two elements could create a new chemical compound, so Romantic poetry could weld different disciplines and subjects into something distinctive and new.[4]

In a statement that links closely to everyday aesthetics, Novalis explains that "By giving the commonplace a higher meaning, by making the ordinary look mysterious, by granting to what is known the dignity of the unknown and imparting to the finite a shimmer of the infinite, I romanticize."[5]

In his *System of Transcendental Idealism*, Friedrich Schelling argues that artwork is an expression of the union between self and nature. Whatever is created by an artist is done through nature. Art is the concrete representation of the infinite found in nature. In such romantic writers and thinkers as Schelling and Schlegel, aesthetic intuition provides humanity to life through immediate access to knowledge of the divine or the absolute. Such a claim moves art to the very center of human existence.[6]

Perhaps the most significant book on aesthetics by the Jena Set was Friedrich Schiller's *On the Aesthetic Education of Man*. Written and published in the form of a series of letters and influenced by A.G. Baumgarten's 1750 book *Aesthetica*, Schiller puts attention on knowledge mediating between upper and lower functions. He claims that the most important clue to human history is that humans are creatures of sense before reason.[7]

For Schiller, what could be better suited to mediate between the perceptions of sense and the insights of reason than art objects? Artwork presents abstractions in sensuous form.

> But since in the enjoyment of beauty, or aesthetic unity, an actual union and interchange between matter and form, passivity and activity, momentarily takes place, the compatibility of our two natures, the practicability of the infinite being realized in the finite, hence the possibility of sublimest humanity, is thereby actually proven.[8]

Schiller views art as a kind of playful, yet profound, interaction between mind and the physical world. He asks: "How can we speak of mere play, when we know that it is precisely play and play alone, which of all man's states and conditions is the one which makes him whole and unfolds both sides of his nature at once?"[9]

The radical thoughts and lifestyles of these romantic groups led to criticism from many different directions. The Danish philosopher Soren Kierkegaard argued that the romantics made art a secular alternative to religion. In this way, romantics are forerunners to the nihilists. In his book *On the Concept of Irony*, Kierkegaard claimed that the romantics had effectively replaced God with the creative human mind.[10]

Yoshimatsu points to the British romantics and the American transcendentalists as movements of thought as having strong parallels to Eastern philosophy. Wordsworth and Coleridge inspired and stimulated their readers to use imagination to see the beauty in the everyday by praising commonplace happenings and changing them into a form of art.[11] As William Blake wrote:

> To see a World in a Grain of Sand
> And a Heaven in a Wild Flower:
> Hold Infinity in the palm of your hand
> And Eternity in an hour. . . . [12]

JOHN DEWEY AND *ART AS EXPERIENCE*

John Dewey is clearly the most influential source for the everyday aesthetics philosophy, particularly through his book *Art as Experience*. Over his lifetime, Dewey wrote sporadically on art, beginning with his first book *Psychology*, in which one chapter addressed "aesthetic feeling." For Dewey, experience is itself aesthetic, and art is the consummation of ordinary experience found everywhere.

In repudiating the art versus life opposition that is common in aesthetic theory, Dewey followed Emerson in objecting to the division of beauty from use as something the laws of nature do not support. Dewey embraced Emerson's ardently democratic vision of art, opposing the exclusionary elitism of high culture. In Dewey's conception, art is not an otherworldly emanation channeled by a uniquely talented artist, but rather a product of natural forces engaged in our cultural context. Consequently, art is not pursued purely for its own sake but for a more fulfilling life.[13]

This approach contradicts an aesthetics focused on uniquely talented artists, and detailed delineations separating great from good art, what Dewey terms the "museum concept of art." For him, the best art is also the best experience. Art is not an imitation of an action or people, nor a substitute for experience, but rather a quality that permeates daily experience.[14]

Dewey contends in his description of "having an experience" that aesthetic involvement is possible in every aspect of one's daily life. By locating beauty in the character of an experience rather than in a specific kind of object or situation, Dewey paves the way for subsequent everyday aesthetics advocates to explore diverse aspects of people's lives without a pre-configured boundary. In this way, aesthetics is an attitude of living.[15]

Dewey presents a grand vision of human history with central roles for democratic faith and aesthetics in interaction with nature. He sees a "continuous human community" leading up to the present, leaving the living with an immense responsibility to make the cultural riches more "widely accessible and more generously shared"—not confined to specific class or race.

Dewey seems to have in mind a Darwinian evolutionary reasoning for linking art and experience:

> Because experience is the fulfillment of an organism in its struggles and achievements in a world of things, it is art in germ. Even in its rudimentary forms, it contains the promise of that delightful perception which is esthetic experience.[16]

In this way, the seemingly ordinary can elicit a stronger aesthetic experience than those set apart as formal art objects: "Even a crude experience, if authentically an experience, is more fit to give a clue to the intrinsic nature of esthetic experience than is an object already set apart from any other mode or experience."[17]

Writing in a manner that is reminiscent of Nietzsche's *Birth of Tragedy*, Dewey describes a process of recognition and reflection in the interaction of the viewer with the art object: "Art celebrates with peculiar intensity the moments in which the past reenforces the present and in which the future is a quickening of what now is."[18] Dewey's notion is that the aesthetic viewer turns life on itself:

> Ultimately there are but two philosophies. One of them accepts life and experience in all its uncertainty, mystery, doubt, and half-knowledge and turns that experience upon itself to deepen and intensify its own qualities—to imagination and art. This the philosophy of Shakespeare and Keats.[19]

Dewey argues that despite the common notion of the product of art as being an object, it is an experience: "The product of art—temple, painting, statue, poem—is not the work of art. The work takes place when a human being cooperates with the product so that the outcome is an experience that is enjoyed because of its liberating and ordered properties."[20]

As seen earlier with some of the German philosophers, this philosophical shift moves the focus of aesthetics from the artist and the artwork to the viewer. The observer then becomes an active participant in an interactive experience. Furthermore, this experience is, like the communal Greek theater performances, intensely collective.

> Art is the extension of the power of rites and ceremonies to unite men, through a shared celebration, to all incidents and scenes of life. This office is the reward and seal of art. The art weds man and nature is a familiar fact. Art also renders men aware of their union with one another in origin and destiny.[21]

Furthermore, Dewey connects spirituality to art, and he lays claim to the possibility for spiritual experiences outside of formal religion, insisting that mystical experiences are part of daily human experience:

> There is no reason for denying the existence of experiences that are called mystical. On the contrary, there is every reason to suppose that, in some degree of intensity, they occur so frequently that they may be regarded as normal manifestations that take place at certain rhythmic points in the movement of experience.[22]

He pointedly rejects that religions monopolize spirituality and argues that in some ways they stand in the way of individuals accessing religious values discovered in ordinary human experience.

Aesthetic spirituality describes one variety of the secular spiritual quest in the American grain that Dewey and William James represent. Secular spirituality could play an active role in the lives of even those individuals who find themselves alienated from churches or synagogues but still open to what William James called "the More," and John Dewey the "religious quality of experience."[23]

Dewey disavows any dichotomy between God and nature and attempts to show that supernatural principles are grasped through nature's processes. This pragmatist spirituality could be achieved in a variety of ways, including poetic inspiration, philosophical reflection, and devotion to a noble cause. The self, according to Dewey, is always directed toward something beyond itself, and any work of art could be described as eliciting a sense of belonging to the all-inclusive whole.[24]

The individual by standing in a right relation to things may be visited by a sense of "sublimity." Although contact with infinite and eternal reality is the apotheosis of consciousness, our most immediate access to it may be through an embrace of our embodied nature. It is through the creation and appreciation of art that our capacity for freedom from personal interest is grounded in material reality.[25]

As human experience is situated in historical, social, and political contexts, defining art as experience ensures that these contexts are given the attention deserved rather than isolating the aesthetic in a narrow formalism. By maintaining that aesthetic experience holds the key to understanding all experience, Dewey could effectively claim that despite the repeated critiques that his philosophy is one-sidedly scientific, the aesthetic lay at the heart of his entire philosophical project because it is fundamental to his experience-centered empiricism.[26]

In Dewey's time, he was not without detractors. For instance, Dewey's former disciple, Randolph Bourne, attacked his philosophy for its lack of "poetic vision." The assault was renewed in the late 1920s, when Lewis Mumford characterized the philosophy of Dewey as acquiescence to capitalist industry. Mumford condemned what he saw as pragmatism's idealization of practical contrivances without comparable interest in artistic imagination.[27]

AESTHETICS OF THE EVERYDAY

Everyday aesthetics refers to the possibility of experiences through what is usually considered non-art objects and events, rejecting distinctions between fine and popular art, art and craft, aesthetic and non-aesthetic experiences. The general argument of this philosophy is that there is an aesthetic dimension to a variety of experiences that are common to all. Everyday aesthetics is first a critique of institutions and practices, and second a focus on non-art objects and modes of experience. Finally, everyday aesthetics incorporates multiculturalism, taking in the conceptions of art and experiences of non-Western cultures.[28]

Two classics of the everyday aesthetics movement are Ben-Ami Scharfstein's *Of Birds, Beasts, and Other Artists*, and Arnold Berleant's *Art and Engagement*. Scharfstein contends that: "We create to remake the world, unite with it more intimately, and become in a measure what we imagine ourselves to be."[29] He sees this process as destructive at first, and then a remaking.

> To rule over things, one must first wrench them from their context and, if necessary, break them up, so as to weaken their resistance to possession, and then perhaps reintegrate them into a world over which one rules with the sense of emotional plenitude that is the opposite of loneliness.[30]

Berleant argues that any attempt to account for art must start from the ways in which art works in human experience. "Engagement" with art is a stance that removes all practical interests and allows us to contemplate the work of art for its own sake:

> Most important for us as creators and appreciators of art is the contribution we ourselves make, a contribution that is active and constitutive. That is why I call this an aesthetics of engagement, a participatory aesthetics.[31]

Berleant claims that much of the previous writing about aesthetics depends on "disinterestedness" in the viewer, requiring the separation of the object from its surroundings in order that it may be contemplated freely. He contends that aesthetic activity is instead a unified process that joins aspects of art and aesthetic appreciation into an inseparable experiential whole in four dimensions: creation, object, appreciation, and performance.

E.H. Gombrich, another major influence on the everyday aesthetics movement, asserts that there is no such thing as "art" per se, only artists.

> Once these were men who took coloured earth and roughed out the forms of a bison on the wall of a cave; today some buy their paints, and design posters for hoardings; they did and do many other things. There is no harm in calling all these activities art as long as we keep in mind that such a word may mean very different things in different times and places, and as long as we realize that Art with a capital A has no existence.[32]

Gombrich seeks to prove that everyone is an artist, in at least a modest way. He gives the example of arranging flowers as an artistic practice:

> Anybody who has ever tried to arrange a bunch of flowers, to shuffle and shift the colours, to add a little here and take away there, has experienced this strange sensation of balancing forms and colours without being able to tell exactly what kind of harmony it is he is trying to achieve.[33]

Everyday aesthetic theory is consistent with many contemporary art forms often full of references to the commonplace. Since the mid-1990s, numerous exhibitions attest to the widespread appeal of the mundane to curators and artists alike.

> For some, this turn to the ordinary leads to a recognition of the dignity of ordinary behavior or the act of stating simply, "here is value." For others, it may result in an unveiling of the "accidentally miraculous," or the desire to make art with the unassuming ease of the amateur photographer.[34]

The everyday is a place where ordinary people creatively use and transform the world they encounter daily.

Yuriko Saito, one of the leading scholars writing about the aesthetics of everyday life, in summarizing the development of the field, notes that in the history of Western aesthetics, originally the subject matters that received attention ranged from natural objects and utilitarian objects. However, beginning with the 19th century, the discourse became increasingly focused on the fine arts. This narrowing attention occurred despite the prominence of the aesthetic attitude theory in modern aesthetics, according to which there is virtually no limit to what can become a source of aesthetic experience. Challenges to this rather limited scope of aesthetics began during the latter half of the 20th century with a renewed interest in nature and the environment, followed by the exploration of popular arts. Everyday aesthetics continues this widening scope by including objects, events, and activities that constitute people's daily life.[35]

For Saito, the aesthetic appreciation of everyday life requires defamiliarization. Because we are most of the time preoccupied by the task at hand in our daily lives, practical considerations mask the aesthetic potential of commonplace objects and ordinary activities. Furthermore, such experiences lack any coherent structure consisting of unity, pervasive character, and a clear beginning and an end.[36]

According to this interpretation, what is new about everyday aesthetics is its illumination of those aspects of our lives that are normally neglected or ignored because they are eclipsed by standout experiences we often have with works of art and nature. More careful attention and a different mindset can reveal a surprisingly rich aesthetic dimension of the otherwise mundane, non-memorable, ordinary parts of our daily life.[37]

In her important book, *The Aesthetics of the Familiar: Everyday Life and World-making*, Saito notes that everyday aesthetics is a subdiscipline of aesthetics, but points out that the original Greek meaning included many dimensions of life in the term's meaning.

> I think it is a mistake to limit what counts as the legitimate ingredients of everyday life for everyday aesthetics discourse: life does not come in neat packages of

different experiences and everyday aesthetics should embrace its complexities with all the messiness created by them.[38]

To be put in the foreground as an object of aesthetics, it must be illuminated in some way to render it out-of-the-ordinary, unfamiliar, or strange: it needs to be defamiliarized. Because aesthetic sensibility requires that we overcome our normal attitudes, it is an open-mindedness.

> Thus, one way of facilitating everyday aesthetics is to focus on these moments or pockets of pleasurable experience that otherwise do not get attention because they become absorbed into the background of our life. The assumption underlying all of these claims is that once we adopt an appropriate mindset and cultivate a sharper aesthetic sensibility, whether it be through an artistic lens or a Zen-like stance, positive aesthetic values can be found, or constructed in almost every aspect of everyday life.[39]

Saito notes that one value of cultivating everyday aesthetic sensibility is to sharpen one's awareness toward what otherwise escapes our attention due to habitual experience and to nurture open-mindedness, which contributes to a more mindful way of living: "I propose that one mission of everyday aesthetics is to raise our awareness of this power of the aesthetic and develop what may be called aesthetic literacy."[40]

As shown in the previous chapter, one of the most important findings of comparative aesthetics is that a greater emphasis is placed on everyday life in many non-Western cultures than in the West. However, Saito claims that because everyday aesthetics was initially proposed as a way of overcoming modern Western aesthetics' limitations, its scope as a discipline has not been clearly defined.[41] Saito notes that art-centered aesthetics tend to focus on how art objects different from non-art objects and experiences. Aesthetics are then defined by how something is like art. Another key art-centered aesthetic bias is toward objects that have permanence, rather than a focus on process and transience. She maintains that everyday aesthetics needs to be pursued because it expands art-based aesthetics into the everyday life, enriches aesthetic discourse, and impacts the quality of life because traditional art experiences are rare for most people.

Similarly, Irvin claims that if aesthetic experience really was restricted to encounters with art and nature, those who live and work in urban environments that are not very art-infused live lives that are lacking. He argues that everyday life has an aesthetic character that is available at every moment.

> The neglect of the domain of the everyday within the discipline of aesthetics is unfortunate, for this domain offers the prospect of significant satisfactions that are different in character form those available from experiences of art and

nature, and that do not require travel to art galleries, nature preserves or other special sites.[42]

In the design field, most people don't regularly encounter fine art, whereas designed objects are engaged daily by all. Design is defined as functional, immanent, mass-produced, and mute. The product of the design process is an intentionally functional object that is thereby distinguished as a kind of thing, as is further original or individual based on its apparent or formal features.[43]

Design is important to us because it is embedded in daily life. A preoccupation with the fine arts has usually left design out of the aesthetic discussion. An aesthetics of design functions as a corrective to this trend and offers an avenue both for broadening the scope of aesthetic inquiry and for reintegrating aesthetic theory into philosophy. However, he warns that there is a risk of trivializing everyday aesthetics if open to pleasure, comfortable, delicious as criteria.

Joseph H. Kupfer, in his influential book *Experience as Art: Aesthetics in Everyday Life*, focuses on aesthetics and incompleteness.

> The aim of the book is to call into question our ordinary experience, enlivening in the reader a sense of its aesthetic potential, implications, and—finally—its incompleteness. The temporal incompleteness threatened by death; the social incompleteness risked in sex and uncovered in violence; and the cognitive incompleteness necessary to learning. The felt quality, the *aisthesis* of such everyday incompleteness, must be ultimately substantiated by the reader.[44]

In fact, he sees learning itself as an aesthetic experience because of its qualities of searching and use of dramatic structure. Kupfer claims that Plato's dialogues are a perfect example of the aesthetics of learning seen in a dramatic form described as "pedagogical dramas."[45]

The emergence of everyday aesthetics discourse parallels the increasing attempt at blurring the distinction between art and life in today's art world. Although there have been many examples throughout art history of depicting slices of everyday life, 20th-century art introduced and experimented with different modes of appropriating everyday life, most famously with the use of ready-mades.

Artists have been trying to overcome the presumed separation between art and real life in several ways by rejecting the art institutional setting as a location for their art and denying the necessity of expert authority. Additionally, artists embrace various accidental changes to their work, and they encourage the blurring the line between artist and audience.

CONCLUSION

In this chapter, major philosophers and movements in thinking about aesthetics were profiled, from German romantics to the American transcendentalists. With the pragmatism of John Dewey, then heavily braced by an increasing understanding of world art in the modern era, aesthetics as a discipline evolved to its current more sophisticated appreciation of beauty in everyday life. Saito points to the quality-of-life improvement for those embracing everyday aesthetics.

A challenge for the further development of everyday aesthetics is one of clarification and categorization. Is everything one experiences a potential aesthetic experience? Are there differences in degree of effectiveness? Furthermore, what are the implications for artists working with a broader understanding of art? How do discipline, skill, and technical training fit in with everyday aesthetics? Overall, what needs to be explored further is the nuances of this philosophic approach.

In the next two chapters, the discussion turns to first digital, then biological art. Now armed with an understanding of how aesthetics developed, the reader is better prepared to consider the new artwork created with rapidly advancing technology. What is art? Who is an artist? With the philosophy of everyday aesthetics, one sees the contemporary evolution of thinking enlarging the notion of art and beauty. Biological and computer art make concrete the contentions of everyday aesthetics and provide new avenues and instruments for creative expression and appreciation.

NOTES

1. Armstrong, J. (2005). *The secret power of beauty: Why happiness is in the eye of the beholder*. London, UK: Penguin Books.

2. Armstrong, J. (2005). *The secret power of beauty: Why happiness is in the eye of the beholder*. London, UK: Penguin Books, p. 6.

3. Wulf, A. (2022). *Magnificent rebels: The first Romantics and the invention of the self*. New York: Alfred A. Knopf.

4. Wulf, A. (2022). *Magnificent rebels: The first Romantics and the invention of the self*. New York: Alfred A. Knopf, p. 164.

5. Wulf, A. (2022). *Magnificent rebels: The first Romantics and the invention of the self*. New York: Alfred A. Knopf, p. 164.

6. Wulf, A. (2022). *Magnificent rebels: The first Romantics and the invention of the self*. New York: Alfred A. Knopf. ; Pattison, G. (1991). *Art, modernity and faith: Towards a theology of art*. New York: St. Martin's Press.

7. Wilkinson, E.M., & Willoughby, L.A. (eds.). (1982). *Friedrich Schiller on the aesthetic education of man: In a series of letters*. Oxford, UK: Oxford University Press.

8. Wilkinson, E.M., & Willoughby, L.A. (eds.) (1982) *Friedrich Schiller on the aesthetic education of man: In a series of letters*. Oxford, UK: Oxford University Press, p. 189.

9. Wilkinson, E.M., & Willoughby, L.A. (eds.) (1982) *Friedrich Schiller on the aesthetic education of man: In a series of letters*. Oxford, UK: Oxford University Press, p. 105.

10. Pattison, G. (1991). *Art, modernity and faith: Towards a theology of art*. New York: St. Martin's Press.

11. Yoshimatsu, J. (2011). The art in the everyday: A spiritual journey of aesthetic experience within western and Japanese contexts (Order No. 3484380). Available from ProQuest Central; Publicly Available Content Database. (903257084). Retrieved from http://ezproxy.lapl.org/login?url=https://www.proquest.com/dissertations-theses/art-everyday-spiritual-journey-aesthetic/docview/903257084/se-2.

12. Blake, W. "Auguries of Innocence."

13. Shusterman, R. (2010). Dewey's Art as Experience: The Psychological Background. *Journal of Aesthetic Education*, 44(1): 26–43.

14. Martin, J. (2002). *The education of John Dewey: A biography*. New York: Columbia University Press.

15. Dewey, J. (1934). *A common faith*. New Haven, CT: Yale University Press.

16. Dewey, J. (1934b). *Art as experience*. New York: The Berkley Publishing Group, p. 19.

17. Dewey, J. (1934b). *Art as experience*. New York: The Berkley Publishing Group, p. 9.

18. Dewey, J. (1934b). *Art as experience*. New York: The Berkley Publishing Group, p. 17.

19. Dewey, J. (1934b). *Art as experience*. New York: The Berkley Publishing Group, p. 35.

20. Dewey, J. (1934b). *Art as experience*. New York: The Berkley Publishing Group, p. 222.

21. Dewey, J. (1934b). *Art as experience*. New York: The Berkley Publishing Group, p. 282.

22. Dewey, J. (1934). *A common faith*. New Haven, CT: Yale University Press, p. 35.

23. Van Ness, P.H. (1996). *Spirituality and the secular quest*. New York: The Crossroad Publishing Company.

24. Van Ness, P.H. (1996). *Spirituality and the secular quest*. New York: The Crossroad Publishing Company.

25. Van Ness, P.H. (1996). *Spirituality and the secular quest*. New York: The Crossroad Publishing Company.

26. Shusterman, R. (2010). Dewey's Art as Experience: The Psychological Background. *Journal of Aesthetic Education*, 44(1): 26–43.

27. Shusterman, R. (2010). Dewey's Art as Experience: The Psychological Background. *Journal of Aesthetic Education*, 44(1): 26–43.
28. Sartwell, C. (2003). Aesthetics of the everyday. In Levinson, J., *The Oxford handbook of aesthetics*. Oxford, UK: Oxford University Press.
29. Scharfstein, B. (1988). *Of birds, beasts, and other artists: An essay on the universality of art*. New York: New York University Press, p. 81.
30. Scharfstein, B. (1988). *Of birds, beasts, and other artists: An essay on the universality of art*. New York: New York University Press, p. 2.
31. Berleant. A. (1991). *Art and engagement*. Philadelphia, PA: Temple University Press, p. 4.
32. Gombrich, E.H. (1996). *The essential Gombrich*. London, UK: Phaidon, p. 65.
33. Gombrich, E.H. (1996). *The essential Gombrich*. London, UK: Phaidon, p. 75.
34. Johnstone, S. (ed) (2008). *The everyday: Documents of contemporary art*. Boston, MA: MIT Press, p. 12.
35. Saito, Y. (2021). Aesthetics of the Everyday. *The Stanford encyclopedia of philosophy* (Spring 2021 Edition), Edward N. Zalta (ed.), https://plato.stanford.edu/archives/spr2021/entries/aesthetics-of-everyday/.
36. Saito, Y. (2021). Aesthetics of the Everyday. *The Stanford encyclopedia of philosophy* (Spring 2021 Edition), Edward N. Zalta (ed.), https://plato.stanford.edu/archives/spr2021/entries/aesthetics-of-everyday/.
37. Saito, Y. (2021). Aesthetics of the Everyday. *The Stanford encyclopedia of philosophy* (Spring 2021 Edition), Edward N. Zalta (ed.), https://plato.stanford.edu/archives/spr2021/entries/aesthetics-of-everyday/.
38. Saito, Y. (2017). *Aesthetics of the familiar: Everyday life and world-making*. Oxford, UK: Oxford University Press, p. 11.
39. Saito, Y. (2017). *Aesthetics of the familiar: Everyday life and world-making*. Oxford, UK: Oxford University Press, p. 19.
40. Saito, Y. (2017). *Aesthetics of the familiar: Everyday life and world-making*. Oxford, UK: Oxford University Press, p. 186.
41. Saito, Y. (2021). Aesthetics of the Everyday. *The Stanford encyclopedia of philosophy* (Spring 2021 Edition), Edward N. Zalta (ed.), https://plato.stanford.edu/archives/spr2021/entries/aesthetics-of-everyday/.
42. Irvin, S. (2019). The pervasiveness of the aesthetic in ordinary experience. In Lamarque, P., & Olsen, S.H. (eds.) *Aesthetics and the philosophy of art: The analytic tradition*. Hoboken, NJ: Wiley Blackwell, p. 700.
43. Forsey, J. (2016). *The aesthetics of design*. Oxford, UK: Oxford University Press.
44. Kupfer, J.H. (1983). *Experience as art: Aesthetics in everyday life*. Albany, NY: State University of New York Press, p. 7.
45. Kupfer, J.H. (1983). *Experience as art: Aesthetics in everyday life*. Albany, NY: State University of New York Press, p. 38.

Chapter 4

Digital Art

Three things are changing to upend traditional 19th-century notions of aesthetics. In addition to questioning the definition of art and an awareness of non-Western forms, computers and biotechnology are forcing a conceptual change in thinking about the creative arts.

As detailed in the first chapter, creativity is generally considered a uniquely human activity. While nature is often held up as an aesthetic model to imitate, it is not considered creative in ways parallel to human artistic activity. The idea of making art with technology provokes many, let alone the notion that computers are in any way artistic.

Increasingly, scientists and artists contend that creativity is not limited to humans. This notion is a conviction in varying degrees for many of the scientists and artists working in both computer and biological art. Although creating art using artificial intelligence techniques is relatively new, artists have been using algorithms, automation, and computation to create art for decades. Applications now effectively employ AI to create images and text based on simple prompts requiring no computer programming knowledge. One scholar summarizes the remarkable changes by comparing the present to the time of British artist Harold Cohen's pioneering work using a computer program he developed known as AARON to create art:

> Whereas Harold Cohen worked on his software AARON for decades, it is now possible for a high-school student to generate highly convincing computer-generated paintings using open source code and data sets found online. This evolution of the algorithms has also resulted in new possibilities for generative art.[1]

Blaise Agüera y Arcas, the leader of Google's Seattle AI group and founder of the Artists and Machine Intelligence program, argues that the transformation of artistic practice and theory began with the 19th-century photography revolution, and it is parallel to the current revolution in machine intelligence.

He sees the upheaval as promising to democratize the means of production of art.[2]

Agüera y Arcas further contends that art has always had an evolving relationship to technologies and been constrained by them. AI is a technology that profoundly impacts art:

> As with these earlier innovations, it will ultimately transform society in ways that are hard to imagine from today's vantage point; in the nearer term, it will expand our understanding of both external reality and our perceptual and cognitive processes.[3]

Agüera y Arcas claims that in recent years, approaches to machine intelligence based on approximating the brain's architecture brought important results through deep learning creating a renaissance in artificial neural networks. He asks, what new kinds of art become possible when we begin to play with technology that is analogous not only to the eye, but also to the brain?[4]

Computer art has a fragmented history, at times focusing on technology over important cultural contexts. Yet machines provide a way of scientifically studying art in mathematical/logical terms. The field of experimental aesthetics grew from the analysis of the creative process, attempting to reveal the secrets of art. Scholars considering how visual arts and computer technology could complement and assist each other in new and emerging interdisciplinary areas is known by various terminology such as computational aesthetics and aesthetic computing.[5]

Can computers be creative? What is a computer's creativity like? If the brain is a type of computer, then can computers create in similar ways? Furthermore, should computers be considered active collaborators, not just tools? As presented earlier, many philosophers concentrate on human consciousness as a key aspect of both the creation and appreciation of art. If computers learn artistic techniques like humans, are they artists?

This chapter looks at past, current, and future perspectives of digital art. A synthesis of aesthetics previously presented in this book is applied to this emerging genre. Note that specific artists, scientists, computer applications, and artworks are referenced as examples of movements and trends and are not meant to be exhaustive but to identify patterns and trends.

The phrase "digital art" is used broadly here, encompassing technologies used in various visual and performing arts. The reader will see that artists range greatly in how technologies are used: as a medium, a tool, a collaborator. Furthermore, there are blurred lines among categories of digital and biological art, with some artists employing a combination of both approaches. In the next chapter, a profile of the rise of biological art reveals parallels to digital art.

ORIGINS

The origins of computer-based art arise from a diverse cross-disciplinary and international group of artists and scientists. Some of these important figures were individual artists, others were university- and research laboratory–based scientists (Bell Laboratories and MIT were especially important). The aesthetic theory evolved as the technologies rapidly developed after the Second World War and visionaries began to discuss the synergies of combining the technology and the arts.

The hypothesis that human thought processes are innately simple emerged from the information-processing research of the 1950s and 1960s and was extended especially by Herbert A. Simon. The Nobel Prize–winning economist influenced a range of fields with his notion of "bounded rationality," contending that human beings achieve only a very limited rationality, and as one consequence are prone to identify strongly with subgoals.

> Human beings, viewed as behaving systems, are quite simple. The apparent complexity of our behavior over time is largely a reflection of the complexity of the environment in which we find ourselves.[6]

According to this theory, our success as a species is based on comprehending models of the complex relations and interactions in our environment.

> This is the task of natural science: to show that the wonderful is not incomprehensible, to show how it can be comprehended—but not to destroy wonder. For when we have explained the wonderful, unmasked the hidden pattern, a new wonder arises at how complexity was woven out of simplicity. The aesthetics of natural science and mathematics is at one with the aesthetics of music and painting—both inhere in the discovery of a partially concealed pattern.[7]

If, as Simon contends, that both science and art behave by discernable patterns, might not machines be programmed for artistic purposes?

As seen in the second chapter, the fascination with patterns has a long tradition in both Western and non-Western cultures. Pythagoras believed the world was beautiful because there was a certain measure, proportion, order, and harmony among all elements. Early computer artworks were frequently based on the golden ratio, Fibonacci numbers, and many other concepts characteristic of Pythagorean theory.[8]

Some scholars argue that creativity comes about with restraints, yet randomness and unpredictability play a key role as well. Randomization in art has an extensive history as seen in the Dadaists and other movements throughout the 20th century before use in computer art and is in some ways the key method for making computers creative.[9] At the core of computer programming lies the concept of the algorithm: a sequence of instructions carried out to transform input to an output.[10] Digital art created with the use of algorithms often employing a degree of randomness became one prominent type of computer-based digital art.

One of the most prominent algorithmic artists was Harold Cohen, a well-known 20th-century painter and academic. His long-standing preoccupation with the psychology of art led to his work on computer art. While at the University of California at San Diego, Cohen created AARON, a computer program designed to produce art autonomously.

AARON randomly assembled shapes and colors and body parts to create images. It was unique in that it had a special awareness of where it was located and what remained to be completed on a flatbed plotter. Viewers typically commented that the machine seemed to have sentience as the pen would pause and seem to think about what to draw next. Nevertheless, AARON was not adventurous, but rather like an artist who finds a style and sticks to it.[11]

Bell Laboratory (Bell Labs) was home to some of the most significant breakthroughs in science and engineering from the 1920s to the 1980s. Transistors, lasers, satellites, cellular telephony, and information theory all originated there. Bell Labs also became a crucial site for the juncture among modern art, science, and technology, and the S-C 4020 microfilm plotter was at the heart of the intersection.[12]

A result of the emphasis that Bell Labs placed on interdisciplinarity, artists were able to access equipment that was far more expensive than anything they could afford by themselves, and conversely their presence led scientists to think more expansively. In the history of computer visualization and computational media aesthetics, the importance of Bell Labs and the work of scientists and artists there is well established.[13]

Computer-Generated Pictures was the title of the groundbreaking exhibition held at the Howard Wise Gallery in New York in 1965, the first exhibition of digital art in the United States. The display showcased the work done at Bell Labs, especially that of Béla Julesz, an experimental psychologist focused on visual perception, and A. Michael Noll, an engineer working on speech data—both interested in computer visualization. Bell Labs as an institution was at first unsure how much to link themselves to this new experimental art form.[14]

Noll was one of the first to argue strongly that computers could be more than mere tools for artists: "In the computer, man has created not just an inanimate tool but an intellectual and active creative partner that, when fully exploited, could be used to produce wholly new art forms and possibly new esthetic experiences."[15]

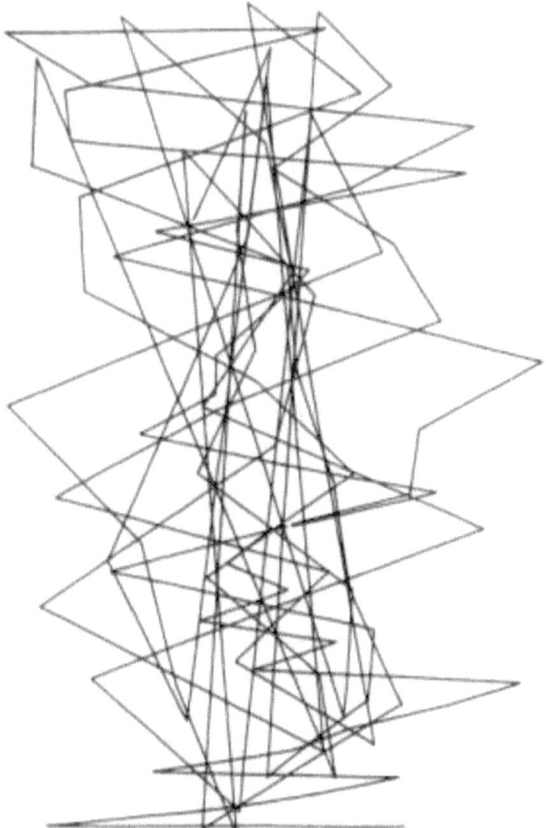

Figure 4.1. *Gaussian-Quadratic*. A. Michael Noll, 1965, *Gaussian Quadratic*, 1962. Ninety-nine lines connect one hundred points whose horizontal coordinates are Gaussian. Vertical coordinates increase according to a quadratic equation. As a point reaches the top, it is reflected to the bottom to continue its rise. The exact proportions of this pattern were chosen from many other examples. This particular proportion is vaguely similar to the painting *Ma Jolie* by Picasso.

Frieder Nake and Georg Nees also created geometric patterns with computers in the 1960s at Bell Labs. Nake began each series by producing a square matrix and filled it with numbers. The matrix was then multiplied succesively with each number was assigned a visual sign with a particular form and color.[16]

Antagonism to computer art came about partially because the technology originated in the military-industrial laboratories. Bell Lab administration tried to disassociate itself from computer art by forcing scientists such as Noll to apply for copyright on their own at the Library of Congress. At first, the Library of Congress refused to copyright Noll's work because it was created by a computer, but then relented when informed a human programmed the computer.[17]

Another root of computer art is from the Manhattan Project's New Mexico Sandia National Laboratory in the Albuquerque area. After the war, Albuquerque blossomed economically, and computer science was part of the Engineering program at the University of New Mexico. The university eventually became a leader in computer art made with the application known as "Art1."

Charles Mattox was an interdisciplinary leader at the University of New Mexico who made sound and kinetic sculptures and worked closely with Richard Williams from the Computer Science Department. Mattox was one of several California artists who came to the University of New Mexico in the 1960s. Williams wrote the Art1 application for an IBM 360 computer, enabling artists who knew nothing about programming to create artworks on the large mainframe machine. Artists in Albuquerque, Minneapolis, and Southern England made hundreds of works with the application.[18]

MIT is perhaps the overall leader in creating synergies between technology and the arts. In 1947, György Kepes at the School of Architecture and Planning at MIT initiated a program in visual design that later became the Center for Advanced Visual Studies, where he served as a director until 1972. An abstract artist, he began to use devices such as X-ray machines, stroboscopic photography, electron microscopes, sonar, radar, high-powered telescopes, and infrared sensors to create images. An exhibition of such images evolved into an influential book titled *The New Landscape in Art and Science*, in which abstract artwork was paired with scientific images. Kepes's center, artwork, and scholarship had a profound influence on the developing field combining technology and the arts.[19]

Blakinger, in his book *Undreaming the Bauhaus*, contends that in the Cold War era Kepes and other artists with an appreciation of science faced the key question: "What is the purpose of art in a brave new world dominated by science and technology? . . . Could the power of the arts, as a transformative force, change science and technology for the better?"[20]

According to Blakinger, Kepes developed at MIT a new paradigm for aesthetic practice—the artist as technocrat. Indeed, Kepes himself was the foremost artist-technocrat, the first artist to join MIT as tenured faculty. He edited a series of extraordinary books on various aspects of science and art collaboration and curated a series of popular public exhibitions.

Kepes was known for wandering the halls of MIT looking for images created by his faculty colleagues in their research. He revealed an entire new world to midcentury viewers combining abstract images with photos of microscopic minerals, the solar system, chemical compounds, and tissue fibers. His 1970 exhibition titled *Exploration* became a blockbuster, the largest in history up to that point at MIT. Later moved to the Smithsonian National Collection of Fine Arts, it drew four times the typical crowd.[21] Figure 4.2 shows a Photo-elastic Walk created by Kepes and William Wainwright that was displayed at the exhibit.

Despite the obvious popularity, art critics were very negative about these exhibits, as they were to art and technology shows at New York galleries, the Los Angeles County Museum of Art (LACMA), and other showcases for computer art. Partly, the criticism was connected to antiwar sentiments, as well as negative views of the growing military-industrial complex links to higher education.[22]

Internationally, Hiroshi Kawano was one of the earliest pioneers of the use of computers in the arts, publishing his first ideas about aesthetics and

Figure 4.2. *Photo-elastic Walk*. Still Image by Nishan Bichajian, 1970. *Photo-elastic Walk* by CAVS Director György Kepes and William Wainwright. MIT Libraries, Cambridge, Massachusetts. Available at http://act.mit.edu/cavs/item/cavs_printbinder _artistsAL_0683

computing in 1962 and computer-generated images in 1964.[23] Kawano changed his approach in the 1970s through his developing interest in artificial intelligence.

In the 1960s, Max Bense with Abraham Moles established new foundations for aesthetics through information theory. Bense coined the terminology of "generative aesthetics" and "artificial art" and became influential across central Europe. He co-founded the Stuttgart School at the *Technische Universitat*, one of the major European centers for research into contemporary aesthetics whose influence continues today.[24]

In terms of formal scholarship, *Leonardo* began publication in Paris in 1968, led by founding editor and kinetic artist Frank Malina, who modeled the journal after the science publications for which he wrote for during his first career in astronautics. Published by MIT Press, *Leonardo* became the popular way of disseminating discussion about computer art.[25] MIT itself continues to be a leader in academic attempts to merge technology and art.

It needs to be pointed out that much of the history of computer science and computer art is dominated by male perspectives. There is an underappreciated role of females in the development of digital art, and the impact of feminist theory on contemporary practice. Women made significant contributions to the aesthetic and practice of digital art and altered digital technology itself. For example, American artist Lillian Schwartz at Bell Labs developed important applications, special color filters and editing techniques, art and historical analyses, art films and graphics that could be viewed in 2D or 3D.[26]

MACHINE LEARNING AND ART

One way to look at the use of computers in art is under the general heading of "machine learning." Audry defines *machine learning* as: "Given a certain kind of task (supervised, unsupervised, or reinforcement learning), a learning algorithm adjusts a model to improve its performance (measured using an evaluation criterion) over a data set."[27] As a field, machine learning strives toward the development of fully autonomous systems that can learn on their own without human intervention and excel in solving difficult problems such as speech recognition and image classification.

Machine learning offers a unique challenge to art because of its historical link to engineering culture. Traditional approaches to art making within computer science and artificial intelligence focus on techniques and outcomes rather than on processes and contexts. Unlike in cognitive science or neuroscience, the aim in machine learning is to build useful systems, not to understand the processes underlying in humans and animals.[28]

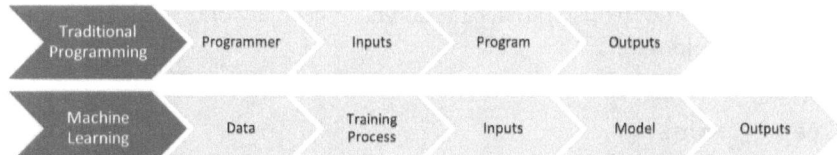

Figure 4.3. Traditional Programming Versus Machine Learning. Based on Audrey, 2021, Fig. 3.3

Learning corresponds to adjusting the values of parameters so that the model matches best with the data it sees during training. Through a particular setting of its parameters learned from the training data, the model becomes specialized to the task that underlies the data. The version of the model developed after training becomes the algorithm for that task. This overall process is termed *computer learning*. The model may be predictive and/or descriptive.[29]

Models exemplify one fundamental concept of machine learning, which is to indirectly design a system by exposing it to examples rather than directly through computer code. As they are trained, models such as genetic programming trees and neural networks self-organize, producing complex representations. "The decision process of these models, which is crystalized in the ways that they are adjusted through the learning procedure, are often surprising and even difficult to interpret by humans."[30]

Some of the key categories of learning machines relevant to art are genetic algorithms, neural networks, and deep learning. Genetic algorithms span a wide family of computer programs that borrow from evolutionary processes attempting to design systems able to learn on their own. Their designs are inspired by how species adapt to their environment through evolutionary principles of reproduction and natural selection. Genetic algorithms have been widely used by artists, composers, and musicians mostly to automate the discovery of interesting new versions.[31]

Richard Dawkins, the evolutionary biologist, is an important influence on the field with his book *The Blind Watchmaker*, in which he describes creating figures by simulating genetics and evolutionary procedures on his computer. Employing several parameters on a treelike structure, Dawkins creates graphic organisms called "biomorphs" subject to artificial selection by a user or artist.[32]

Artificial neural networks are based on a universal black box model in which designers only indirectly control the network by allowing it to learn from data. An important advantage of such approaches over evolutionary algorithms is that they circumvent the need for the system's designer to define a solution using a system of rules. Starting in the 1990s, artists became interested in the properties of artificial neural networks and their capacity to learn directly from real world data. Inspired from biological neural networks models found in nervous systems and brains, these networks lend themselves to artistic explorations.[33]

Deep Learning

Until twenty years ago, it was feasible to train only shallow neural architectures efficiently—that is, neural networks with no more than three layers. A layer in a deep learning model is a structure or network topology in the model's architecture, which takes information from the previous layers and then passes it to the next layer. Deep neural networks consist of more layers and are characterized by greater autonomy, allowing their users to work directly with raw data, thus alleviating the need for the tedious preprocessing typically associated with machine learning. Additionally, these systems extract meaningful information from databases of unprecedented sizes.[34]

In deep learning, the goal is to learn in levels of increasing abstraction with minimum human contribution. It is this extraction of patterns that allows abstraction and learning general descriptions.[35]

> Deep learning promises to expand our senses and to give us access to supreme, planet-broad cognitive capabilities and perception. But as artists explore these systems, they reveal that the imaginary landscapes circulating inside the intricate interconnected units of these neural-inspired models actually mirror our own perceptual processes in all their imperfections.[36]

In this way, the systems are strongly biased, reflecting the limitation of human programmers.

Before deep learning, much of the art created through computer learning were remixes following the basic principles of copy, repeat, and collage. New machine learning technologies such as "deepfakes" push this principle further, expanding the possibilities offered to artists. Deepfakes are images in which a person in an existing image or video is replaced with someone else's likeness.

Machine learning opens the door to entirely new forms of remixes mediated by new models. Computers have been especially successful in imitating artistic styles. For example, two scholars created an application to automatically generate art in the style of Kandinsky during his Bauhaus years. By pseudo-randomizing various parameters the program can make each styled image it generates unique.[37]

Generative Adversarial Networks

In the last few years, the development of Generative Adversarial Networks (GANs) has inspired a wave of algorithmic art using AI in new ways. Generative Adversarial Networks are an approach to modeling using deep learning methods. In contrast to traditional algorithmic art in which the artist writes detailed code that specifies the rules for the desired aesthetics, in GANs the algorithms are set up by the artists to recognize the aesthetics by looking at many images using machine learning technology.[38]

The generative adversarial network is not precisely a deep learning method. The innovation of GAN is in the way the task is defined rather than how it is implemented. The human artist chooses a collection of images, such as traditional art portraits, to feed the algorithm in the pre-curation stage. These images are fed into a generative AI algorithm that tries to imitate the collection of inputs. The algorithm then produces new images that follow the aesthetics learned.[39]

The most widely used GAN introduced by Ian Goodfellow in 2014 employed a dueling-neural-network approach vastly improving learning from unlabeled data.[40] By internalizing the characteristics of a collection of images a GAN can improve the resolution of a pixelated image, create realistic photos, or apply a particular artistic style to a picture. At the end of the process, a human sifts through output images for artistic use. The development of GANs has sparked a new wave of AI art and use in modeling or prototyping.[41]

GANs are based on game theory with two dueling networks: the generator (G) and the discriminator (D), both deep neural networks. G is like an art forger, while D operates like a detective evaluating the images generated by G based on criteria that are layered. The application "learns" by a back-and-forth process.

One leader in the field is Rutgers University's Art & AI Lab AICAN with the stated goal to study the artistic creative process and how art evolves cognitively and perceptually. Its model is based on an evolutionary aesthetic theory proposed by psychologist Colin Martindale simulating how artists digest prior artworks until they break out of established styles and create something new.[42]

According to Martindale, most art and literary historians deny that there are universal laws of art history. In his research, Martindale took a scientific approach in his computerized content analysis employing a huge database searching for key words focused on novelty, complexity, variability, and periods of stylistic change. He found there is a human tendency informing art to appreciate some novelty and dislike too much repetition. On the other hand, too much originality is a bad thing.

We like a bit of novelty occasionally, but not much. We do not care for people who repeat themselves endlessly. We prefer those who say or do somewhat novel things. Anyone who says or does something too novel, though, is ignored or put away.[43]

The process utilizes a Creative Adversarial Network (CAN), a variant of GAN, that uses "stylistic ambiguity" to achieve novelty.[44] The machine is trained between two opposing forces: one training the machine to follow the aesthetics of the art it is shown and minimizing deviation, while the other force corrects the application if it copies an already established style. These two opposing forces ensure that the art generated is novel, but at the same time that it will not depart too much from common aesthetic rules. This approach is called the "least effort" principle in Martindale's theory.[45]

The Rutgers work focuses on understanding the process of creativity to discover a model simulating that by which art is taught. As visual artists are generally taught their métier by closely studying the work of those who came before them, the software is trained on thousands of paintings. The system is designed to encourage choices that deviate from copying to encouraging new combinations based on a knowledge of art styles.[46]

Some scholars argue for a new system for generating art beyond GANs.[47] Phillip Isola and his team invented a variation on GANs called Conditional Generative Adversarial Networks (CGANs). They are conditional because instead of starting from nothing, they condition it by using an actual reference image.[48]

Applications Using Text Prompts to Create Art

One of the most exciting and accessible areas in the use of technologies in the arts is with the use of artificial intelligence for digital art creation based on written text prompts. A prompt is an input to an artificial intelligence application. This software utilizes public domain visual data, often older artworks, and then synthesizes the content and styles to create something new to respond to the text-inputted prompt.[49]

Midjourney and DALL-E (for graphics) and Livebook AI (for text) are at the time of this printing popular applications producing images from text prompts. A video application named Make-a-Video has also been released.[50] Livebook AI is an artificial intelligence system built for writing illustrated stories, blogs, and books in more than two thousand categories and genres.[51] Each application interprets prompts differently, with some accepting images, and varying in restricting parameters for the prompts.

Figure 4.4 is an example of an imagine created by DALL-E2 from the following text prompt: "robot as artist in French countryside field painting with

Digital Art 91

Figure 4.4. Dall-E2 Generated Image

brushes and easel, Impressionist, bright sunshine." DALL-E2 and similar applications are especially productive when given styles and specific color, texture, references to specific artists, backgrounds, moods, and lighting input. There is a strategy in the use of prompts to get effective responses from the software including listing the most important information first.

When images are input into the application, the AI tries to recognize images and then augments it with the additional prompt instructions. Since landscape and building images are readily available as sources, the applications excel in creating scenery and architectural drawings. A key to understanding why certain things turn out well and others don't is knowing what datasets are mostly used in the training of these applications. For instance, artificial intelligence models have access to large amounts of sci-fi data and therefore science fiction scenery and landscapes hold a ready place in artificial intelligence-generated artwork.

Compositions using specific material prompts, such as mosaics and stained glass, work well. Marble and other stones, as well as metals used in prompts produce good results. Adding the third dimension in the prompt makes the resulting illustration more consistent dimensionally, which is sometimes a challenge for AI.

One of the primary uses in the future for this AI software may be to visualize architectural and engineering designs at the conceptual stage. Some of the most famous engineering sketches and designs are well known to AI. According to one expert in the field, the ability of the software to act artistically or in a very detailed engineering manner is impressive: "What fascinates me with A.I. is its ability to be creative as an artist, or precise and focused as a business architect, depending on how you formulate your request in the prompt."[52]

Brett Steele, the dean of UCLA School of the Arts and Architecture, points out that the use of computers is understudied, yet the changes brought about are revolutionary. While much focus has been on the use of computers as a practical tool in architecture, replacing age-old hand tools, some architects are also working with computers as a lead in design. Using forms from nature, geometric forms, and other approaches like those used in the visual arts is likely to be seen in the future.[53]

ROBOTICS

Another area related to computer learning and art is in the use of robots. The origin of machines used in artistic ways comes from "automata," which first appeared in 14th-century Europe, often used in public clocks.

There is a long history of dancers imitating machines. So-called machine ballets followed a theater tradition in which dancers performed conceptions of machinery and commented on them at the same time. Automata, marionettes, and toys come to life are regular occurrences in ballet.[54]

Felicia McCarren, in her book, *Dancing Machines: Choreographies of the Age of Mechanical Reproduction*, describes the history of dancing and robotic movement:

> The science and fiction linking dancers and machines are as old and varied as these conceptions of machines themselves. In scientific traditions, in the literary imagination, and in stage representations, our technologies have often been anthropomorphized by dancers who appear to be simultaneously superhuman in their feats of flexibility and endurance, and subhuman in their wordless physicality. Between machines' not-quite-human functioning and humans' not-quite-machine-like performance, choreographers, philosophers, writers, filmmakers, and artists have situated dancers.[55]

In the early 20th century, a prevalent machine aesthetic in avant-garde movements led to what Martha Graham referred to a decade later as the "omnipresent machine ballets of European dance companies."[56] This trend was partly

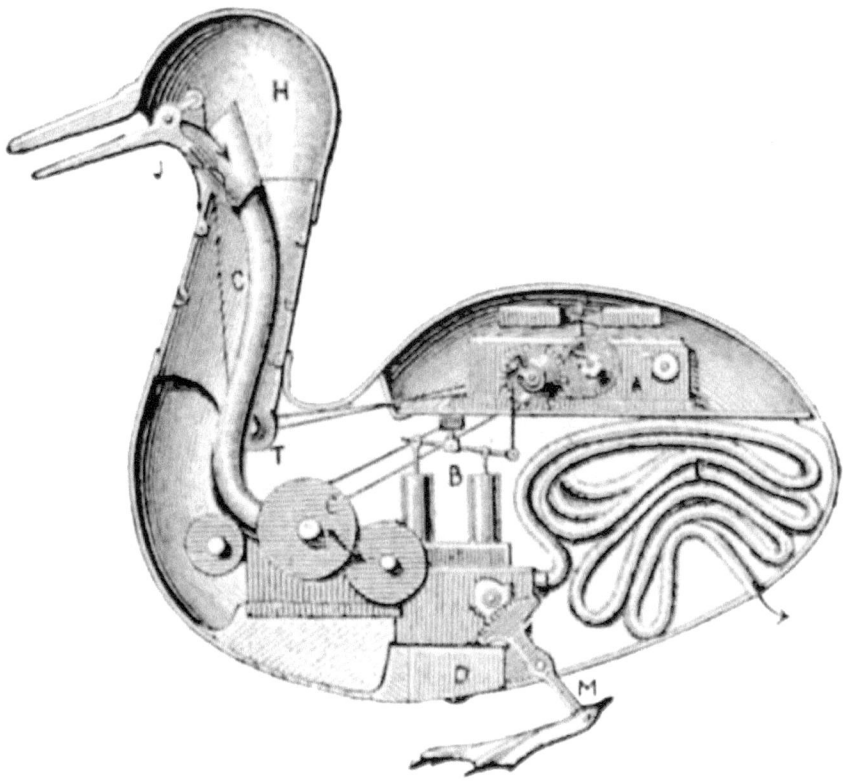

Figure 4.5. A Postulated Interior of the Duck of Vaucanson (1738–1739). Imaginary rendering of Vaucanson's digesting duck in *Scientific American*

inspired by Alfred Jarry's machinical *Ubu Roi* and by performance theory of the first decades of the 20th century, including Craig's *The Actor and the Uber (or Super-) Marionette*. Audiences understood this type of dance as commentary on the human condition in a machine age.

In the second half of the 20th century, New York avant-garde dance in the tradition of Merce Cunningham's early experiments continued to explore the effect of new technologies on dance. Hip-hop and break dancing emerged, also embodying the drive and frenzy of automation. According to McCarren:

> The dancing machine represents both an idealization of the body's performative prowess and a critique of its mechanization, the coordinated precision of rhythmic ensembles and the fragmented but functional isolated gesture of industrial production. It poses the questions of workers' enslavement to technology, or the autonomy and freedom of movement it can bring.[57]

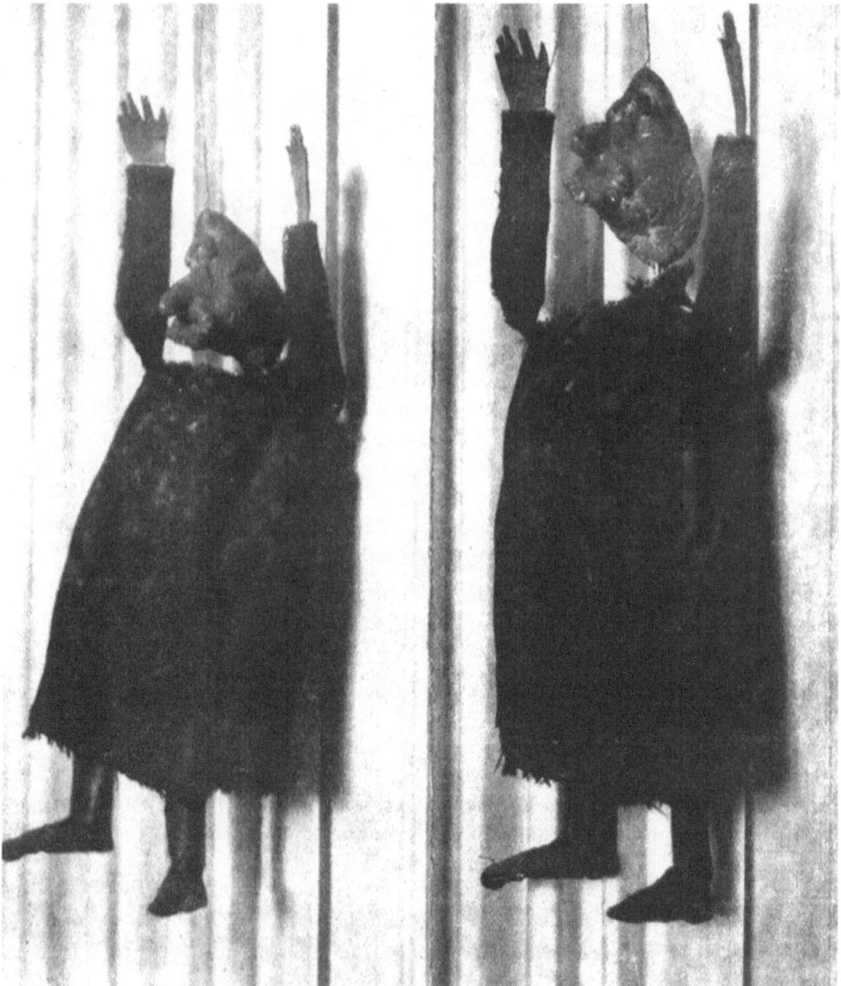

Figure 4.6. Alfred Jarry, Marionnette from the Original Production of *Ubu Roi*. Théâtre de l'Œuvre, December 10, 1896

Contemporary scholars and artists create robots to imitate natural and performance movement. Robotic sculptures use shape-memory alloy motion display technologies to express lifelike movements, such as rustling leaves or squirming tentacles. Works of art combine plant and animal motifs with robotics to give their audience a sense of the objects being alive through their movements. Such projects attempt to explore what it means to feel alive and the mystery of life.[58]

Robocygne is an artistic project that revolves around the development of a custom-built robotic bird, dancing to a remix of Tchaikovsky's Swan Lake.[59]

The artists created the choreography through a process in which movements were programmed into the robot by the choreographer's manipulation of the bird's limbs by hand to the music. To enable this multitracking procedure, the artists in collaboration with engineers developed software that allowed overlaying recording of motions in synchronization with an audio track.[60]

The dance is created by the choreographer manipulating robotic body parts in time with the music. The body consists of two light metal wings with black feathers, a torso of aluminum, black bobbinet, and circuit cards, a vertically adjustable leg, and a flexible neck together with a beak made of eight servo engines.

Stelarc is a well-known "cyborgic" performance artist whose work often involves robotics or other technology integrated with his own body. In one performance, he allowed his body to be controlled remotely by electronic muscle stimulators. Stelarc has also performed with a robotic third arm, and a pneumatic spiderlike, six-legged walking machine that sits the user in the center of the legs and facilitates control of the machine through arm gestures.

His projects and performances are aesthetic gestures to the possibilities of human-machine couplings.

The idea of "collective robotics" appeared in the 1990s from the convergence of the architecture of robots developed by Rodney Brooks with a variety of bio-inspired algorithms focused on new programming tools for solving distributed problems.[61] Bio-inspired algorithms stemmed from the seminal work of Christopher Langton, who launched a new avenue of research in AI

Figure 4.7. Robocygne. Åsa and Carl Unander-Scharin; photo: Elias Lindén

Figure 4.8. Reclining StickMan—2020 Adelaide Biennial of Australian Art. Stelarc; Photographer: Saul Steed

called Artificial Life (aLife) that explores non-biological forms of life. The well-known collective behavior of ants, bees, and other eusocial insects provided the paradigm for the "swarm intelligence" approach of aLife.[62]

The model of swarms of animals and insects in nature is adapted to computer art. Such swarm approaches use the concept in various ways to create computer applications and artworks in coordinated groups. Curators Gary Greenfield and Penousal Machado introduce the works of the artists featured in the Swarm Art Gallery, who explore and engage with the behavioral principles underlying swarms. The development of "swarm art" reveals the broad range of methods that appear within the genre.[63]

While insects communicate among themselves through chemical messages producing certain patterns of collective behavior, Leonel Moura uses color for the swarm of robots to create unique paintings. He argues that recent art history shows many similar examples of artworks based on random procedures. Most important to him is whether a new art form expands the field of art. For Moura, innovation is more important than personal ability.[64]

The question of whether machines can make art on their own provokes very different answers from pioneers in the robotics field. For instance, Harold Cohen refuses to ascribe creativity to his early art-making robot AARON, while Leonel Moura argues that since his Artbots generate pictures from properties that could not have been predicted by their creator, "they

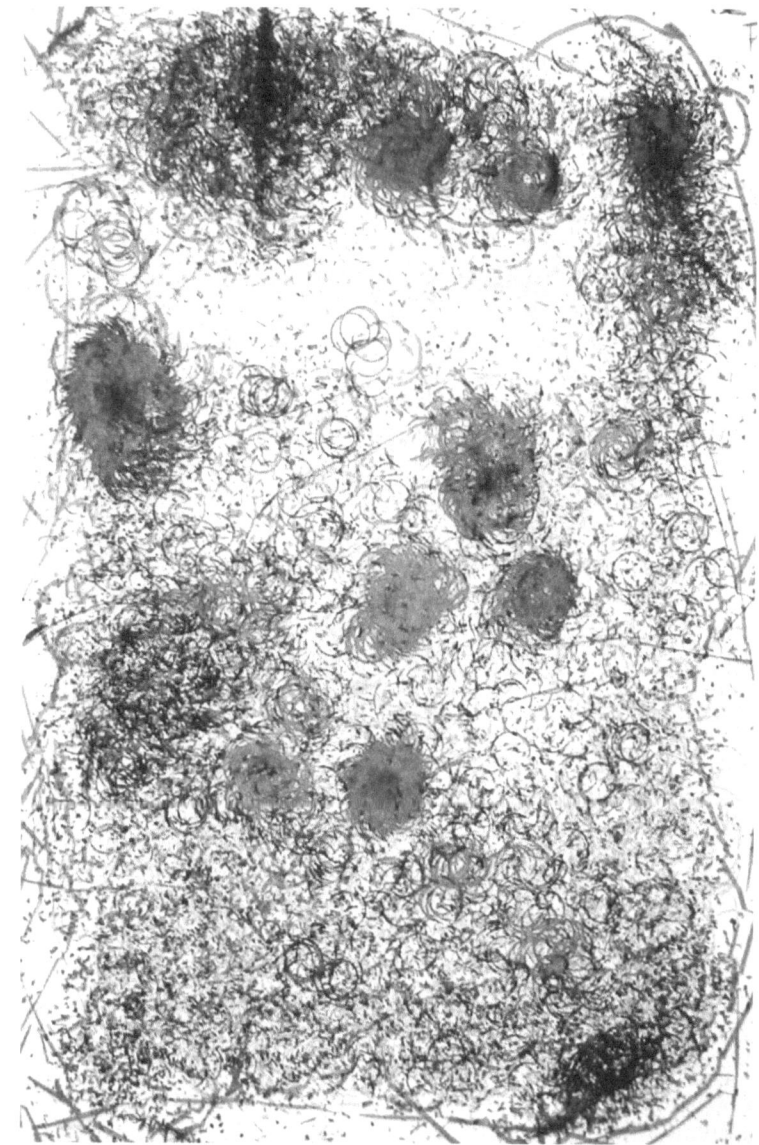

Figure 4.9. Artbots. Leonel Moura

have at least some degree of creativity." Moura contends that the question of whether machines can be artists seems to fall squarely on our definition of "artist." One solution to this question may lie in directing the question to the viewer.[65]

COMPUTERS IN MUSIC AND LITERATURE

Digital music started in the 1970s with the linking of computers to musical instruments, eventually involving composing and improvising functions. Research in engineering departments such as Stanford and MIT led work in computers-based music. One strain of research claimed that computers:

> Opened up the potential for the creative exploration of a much wider range of sounds, enabled the manipulation of timbre to become a highly significant shaping force in music, and facilitated the integration of spatial positioning and movement into musical structure.[66]

The idea was that software can extend the range of those involved in making music, making it more accessible.

Musicians have long been interested in musical games of chance to inform scores, including Bach and Mozart. Music generation is probably one of the most advanced domains of computational creativity. An example is DeepBach, which generates Bach-like choral scores.[67] In an online test with 1,600 listeners, of whom about 25% had significant musical expertise, more than 50% confused scores generated by DeepBach with authentic pieces from the real composer.[68]

In August 2016, the Magenta team at Google released a piece of music they claimed was the first ever to be entirely composed by a computer. The track was created from 4,500 popular tunes and seeded by four musical notes. The computer then created a melody.[69] Magenta uses Google Brain and deep learning with the goal of providing a creative feedback loop for artists in a coevolving way. Magenta is also working on the very difficult AI-programming problem of developing computer humor.

Francois Pachet developed the *Flow Machine* using Markov models that assume that future states depend only on the current state, not on the events that occurred before it, to analyze music and identify patterns to improvise. Music composition applications, as with visual image AI, use large databases of source music to recognize patterns. Mary Farbood, from the MIT Media Lab, created *Hyperscore* linking images to music allowing the user to create music from the images.[70]

Writing computer programs to create literature is difficult because of the complexity of human motivation. The need for background knowledge, and the intricacy of natural language, make the computer literature project very challenging. Yet AI has been used to write stories, blog posts, and technical documentation, as well as make videos and animation. Livebook AI is a system built to simplify story-writing, publishing, and copywriting processes using large language models with prompts such as a title or a genre.[71]

Internationally there have been other efforts to use computers for creating literature. A computer application created by engineers at Future University Hakodate in Japan wrote a short story called "The Day a Computer Writes a Novel." Rafael Perez y Perez created MEXICA, a computer story generator and in 2017 published a book of twenty stories created by the program: "MEXICA: 20 years—20 Stories."[72]

AI may help with drafting various kinds of writing for authors, speeding up the process and providing inspiration. Chatbots are a form of AI receiving quite a bit of attention at the time of writing this book.[73] A chatbot is a software application used typically to conduct online conversations via text in lieu of providing direct contact with a live human agent and are designed to convincingly simulate the way a human would behave as a conversational partner.

Chatbots are used in dialog systems for various purposes including customer service, request routing, or information gathering. While some chatbot applications simply scan for general keywords and generate responses using common phrases obtained from an associated library or database, others use extensive word-classification processes, natural-language processors, and sophisticated AI. While research on effectiveness is early at this time, one study at MIT studied writing done by workers involving marketing, grant writing, data analysis writing and editing tasks, and human resources and found that ChatGPTs make work speedier with no sacrifice in quality and then made it easier to "improve work quickly" using the tool.[74]

To show an example of how chatbots work, the author wrote the following prompt into ChatGPT: "Write an opening paragraph to an Ernest Hemingway short story in which a writer in a Paris garret wonders if a computer could ever replace him."

ChatGPT responded:

The dusty garret in Paris was the perfect place for a writer like Jean-Pierre. It was a place where he could indulge his muse and let his thoughts flow onto the page, uninterrupted. But as he sat there, surrounded by the clatter of his ancient typewriter, Jean-Pierre couldn't help but wonder if his craft was in danger. He had heard rumors of a new invention called a "computer" that could write just as well as any human. Could it be possible, Jean-Pierre wondered, that he was soon to be replaced by a soulless machine?

To explain how it worked, ChatGBT responded to the prompt: "Describe how ChatGPT works to write fiction in the style of Ernest Hemingway." In a five-point description, ChatGBT outlined how it works:

1. Training on Hemingway's style: First, ChatGPT was trained on a large corpus of Ernest Hemingway's writings, including his novels, short stories, and essays. By analyzing the patterns, sentence structures, vocabulary, and tone of his writing, ChatGPT learned to imitate Hemingway's style.
2. Understanding the prompt: To write fiction in Hemingway's style, ChatGPT needs a prompt or a starting point. The prompt could be a theme, a character, a setting, or a plot idea. ChatGPT uses natural language processing techniques to understand the prompt and generate relevant ideas.
3. Generating sentences: Based on the prompt and Hemingway's style, ChatGPT generates sentences that are concise, direct, and use simple language. Hemingway's writing is known for its economy of words, so ChatGPT tries to emulate that by avoiding unnecessary words and phrases.
4. Editing and refining: After generating a set of sentences, ChatGPT reviews and edits them to ensure they are grammatically correct, coherent, and match Hemingway's style. This may involve rearranging words or phrases, adding or deleting words, or adjusting the tone and mood of the writing.
5. Iterating and improving: ChatGPT uses a feedback loop to improve its writing over time. It learns from the corrections and feedback it receives from editors and users, which helps it refine its writing style and generate more accurate and compelling fiction in the style of Ernest Hemingway.[75]

COMPUTERS AND THE PERFORMING ARTS

One scholar contends there were three distinct periods in the history of multimedia performance in the 1910s, the 1960s, and the 1990s. Use of projected images and live performance became common in Berlin and Paris in the second decade of the 20th century. By the 1920s, film projection was incorporated into cabaret and music hall performances internationally. Another early influence on technology and performance is through the Russian constructivism beginning in the 1920s.[76]

Italian Futurists were precursors to digital art in that they tried to synthesize technology and performance. They sought a marriage of art and technology and even created a mathematical formula termed synthetic theater: "Painting + sculpture + plastic dynamism + words-in-freedom + composed noise + architecture = synthetic theatre."[77] The Futurist principle of "divisionism" posited binary multitasking such as now used in computers, and some of the techniques that foreshadowed capture motion effects created digitally.

The composer Richard Wagner was an early proponent of mixed media with his notion of the *Gesamtkunstwerk* (total artwork), which advocated for the unification of theater, music, dance, and the visual arts. His 1849 *The Artwork of the Future* sought a synthesis of art forms and was an early proposed form for audience/user immersion. He suggests building theaters that hide the orchestra and stage wings to avoid taking away possible obstructions from audience involvement.[78]

Antonin Artaud's 1938 *The Theatre and Its Double* argued for a primitivist and spiritualized vision of theater. He coined the term *virtual reality*, a predecessor to notions of immersive reality. In the 1950s, multimedia theater was practiced in Czechoslovakia by Laterna Magika. From 1970 to the end of the 20th century, there was a proliferation of the use of media projections in the performing arts. The inexpensiveness of technology drove this increased use, at least partially. In this way, technology and computers have been philosophically and practically part of the performing arts for many years in diverse ways.

By the last decade of the 20th century, computers began to play an increasing role in performance, especially dance.[79] Robert Lepage, the Builders Association, and George Coates Performance Works surrounded their actors with screens projecting digitally manipulated images. Laurie Anderson and William Forsythe also created interactive performance software and performances.[80]

Notably Merce Cunningham projected images of virtual dancers on stage using motion-capture and animation software. Dancer and choreographer Yacov Sharir at the University of Texas at Austin experiments in the intersection of live performance and technology, collaborating with engineers, programmers, and computer animation artists. Sharir utilizes wearable computers that reacted to dancers' movements, heart rates, and neural signals, projecting them as image and color; immersive 3-D environments; and virtual dance partners.[81]

In 1992, Wayne McGregor founded Random Dance because of a long interest in science and technology, fueling choreography and interdisciplinary collaborations.[82] Studio Wayne McGregor developed close ties to a network of researchers and practitioners in fields such as cognitive science, social anthropology, and software development. The application Becoming was developed by McGregor in conjunction with Marc Downie (OpenEnded Group) and Nick Rothwell (Cassiel) seeking to bridge the digital-physical divide between computer program and human dancer.

McGregor's FAR utilizes a computerized pin board of 3,200 LED lights and draws on a cognitive research process inspired by Diderot's encyclopedia. The piece includes a score by Brian Eno collaborator Ben Frost and visuals by Random International.

Some scholar-artists discuss the possibility of presenting the unique qualities of the human body in contemporary dance practice through tailored digital choreographic objects. Other scholars propose technological systems for delivering movement information from a dance performance using a multisensory approach. Such work builds on previous research into interpreting dance as tactile information for vision-impaired audience members.[83]

Johnson describes an interactive dance theater work entitled Encoded that makes use of motion capture techniques and real-time fluid simulations to create systems intended to support, stimulate, and augment live performance. Findings from a qualitative study of performers' experiences with the system point to the challenges of creating theatrical meaning with interactive systems. Additionally, the impact of large-scale projections can have a negative impact on performers' engagement.[84]

Figure 4.10. FAR, Company Wayne McGregor, 2010. Photo: Ravi Deepres

Libby Heaney is a former quantum scientist who creates interactive art pieces involving moving image works, performances, and interactive experiences. Dr. Heaney's *Out of Touch* piece is a site-specific interactive animation using Instagram stories as a medium that invited viewers to activate the animation through touch.[85]

One scholar compares the irregular and unexpected movements in dance to the variable tempos of cell contraction.[86] Led by Royal Society Research Fellow Dr. David Glowacki, danceroom Spectroscopy began as a way of communicating research in chemical physics to non-specialist audiences. The piece is built using much of the same physics, theories, and equations that research scientists use to study how atoms move. Fusing imaging and molecular physics, danceroom Spectroscopy transforms people into energy fields and lets them wander through the nano-quantum world where they trigger sounds and images.[87]

The technology detects human motion giving rise to coherent structure within the atomic dynamics and turns this into real-time soundscapes. "The result is a real-time immersive and interactive audiovisual molecular dynamics experience for an arbitrary number of users, which doubles as both a scientific simulation, and an aesthetic tool."[88]

According to Dixon, the capabilities of computers in performance raise questions about agency, performative action, creation, and the blurring of types and techniques. It can cause us to rethink artistic communication techniques and paradigms.[89]

Figure 4.11. *Danceroom Spectroscopy.* David R. Glowacki

COMPUTERS AND CONSCIOUSNESS

In 1950, British computer pioneer Alan Turing asked a groundbreaking question for the time, "Can computers think?"[90] He located the challenge as two-part: replicating a child brain and then building an education progress for it. Turing proposed a way to test a machine for intelligence involving a conversation between man and machine through a teleprinter. If after a long conversation, the human believed it was conversing with another human, then the machine's intelligence should be conceded. While this Turing Test has been refuted by many, the possible extent of computer intelligence remains.[91]

Scholars often point to consciousness as a defining characteristic of human beings that is beyond computer capability. In addition to coming to an agreed-upon definition of consciousness and the related terms of self-consciousness and subjectivity, the problem with developing theories is amplified by the lack of hard data. Outside of brain images revealing areas of activity, conscious experience is not directly observable at the physical level.[92]

Some scholars argue that consciousness plays a clear evolutionary role in that it incentivizes survival. Conscious organisms are invested in living in a way that makes continued existence important and valuable. It may have evolved to flexibly tap into all the sources of knowledge that might be relevant to our current needs. In all primates, consciousness initially evolved as a communication device, with the prefrontal cortex and its associated long-distance circuits breaking the modularity of local neuronal circuits and broadcasting information across the entire brain. In humans alone, the power of this communication device was later boosted by a second evolution in the emergence of language.[93]

Other scholars view consciousness as an elaborate functional property and as such is likely to have been selected, across millions of years of Darwinian evolution, because it fulfills a particular operational role. There may be a very good reason why our consciousness condenses sensory messages into a synthetic code, devoid of gaps and ambiguities: such a code is compact enough to be carried forward in time, entering what we usually call "working memory." Working memory and consciousness seem to be tightly related.[94]

Michael Graziano, a professor of neuroscience at Princeton University, in his book *Rethinking Consciousness: A Scientific Theory of Subjective Experience*, suggests that consciousness is an efficient model that is used to make predictions about the behavior of animals and is likely to have evolved long before humans. According to Graziano: "Of all the mental talents that we humans like to brag about—math, language, tool use, and so on—consciousness may be one of the most primitive and least special to us." He points out that scholars writing about the evolution of consciousness tend to emphasize a gradual increase in the complexity of the brain. In the process of evolution, the nervous system became so complex that it gained subjectivity.

Graziano claims that once you start with the proposition that consciousness arises naturally from complex information processing, it's hard not to slip into panpsychism—the belief that everything in the universe is conscious to at least some degree.[95] Panpsychism is an ancient concept that all things have a mind or a mindlike quality. It dates to the earliest days of both Eastern and Western civilizations and has been expressed to some degree by major philosophers such as Spinoza, Leibniz, Goethe, Shelling, Schopenhauer, Nietzsche, Schiller, Peirce, James, and Dewey.

In modern times, Dewey argued in *Experience and Nature* that organic and inorganic objects have comparable qualities of interaction. Pierre Teilhard de Chardin, the Jesuit priest and philosopher, was a leading modern panpsychist who claims that all energy is psychic in nature. This notion of panpsychism has the advantage of avoiding the highly anthropocentric use of "consciousness" with its meaning closely associated with human mental states.[96]

Stanislas Dehaene, chair of experimental cognitive psychology at the Collége de France, Paris, notes the historical murkiness in the use of the term *consciousness*. Yet today the problem of consciousness is at the forefront of neuroscience research because of brain-imaging techniques. Such technology has revealed how brain activity unfolds as a piece of information gains access to consciousness, and how this activity differs during unconscious processing. Comparing these two states reveals markers that the stimulus was consciously perceived.[97] Dehaene contends that what counts as genuine consciousness plays a precise role in selecting, amplifying, and propagating relevant thoughts. As a result, it should become possible to create artificial architectures of electronic chips that mimic the operation of consciousness.

CONCLUSION

This chapter began by asking if computers can be creative, and if so, how? The many examples presented show the range and complexity of responses to this question. While clearly artists use computers as they would brushes and different media, they are also moving increasingly toward computer collaboration.

A Rutgers research group conducted experiments to compare the response of human subjects to computer-generated work versus that of human artists. In a study carried out in early 2017, researchers asked eighteen volunteers to look at hundreds of images and rate them on characteristics such as "novelty," "complexity," and "structure." Some of the images showed paintings created by human artists mixed with computer art. The computer art was generated by new AI algorithms trained on more than eighty thousand paintings from the past few hundred years that had been developed to create new visuals in a variety of styles. The art generated by the algorithm was attributed more often incorrectly to people than to computers.[98]

In 2023, MoMA's *Unsupervised* exhibit is an example of the continuing public interest in combining technology and art. The artist Refik Anadol trained a machine-learning model to interpret the publicly available data of MoMA's collection. It reimagines the history of modern art and considers the future of art. According to Anadol, "I am trying to find ways to connect memories with the future," the artist has said, "and to make the invisible visible."[99]

Figure 4.12. Unsupervised—Machine Hallucinations—MoMA. Refik Anadol, 2022. Data sculpture: custom software, generative algorithm with artificial intelligence (AI), real-time digital animation on LED screen, sound, dimensions variable. Copyright Refik Anadol Studio.

In the next chapter, we turn to perhaps the most challenging new type testing the limits of aesthetics: biological art. While there are some similarities to digital art in terms of blending science and art, biological art pushes the edge of current conceptions of aesthetics and raises ethical questions as well.

NOTES

1. Audry, S. (2021). *Art in the age of machine learning.* Cambridge, MA: MIT Press, p. 113.
2. Blaise Agüera, y. A. (2017). Art in the age of machine intelligence. *Arts*, 6(4): 18. doi:https://doi.org/10.3390/arts6040018.
3. Blaise Agüera, y. A. (2017). Art in the age of machine intelligence. *Arts*, 6(4): 18. doi:https://doi.org/10.3390/arts6040018.
4. Blaise Agüera, y. A. (2017). Art in the age of machine intelligence. *Arts*, 6(4): 18. doi:https://doi.org/10.3390/arts6040018.
5. Taylor, G.D. (2014). *When the machine made art: The troubled history of computer art.* London, UK: Bloomsbury ; Zhang, K., Harrell, S. & Ji, X. (2012). Computational aesthetics: On the complexity of computer-generated paintings. *Leonardo*, 45(3): 243–248. doi: https://doi.org/10.1162/LEON_a_00366.
6. Simon, H.A. (2019). *The sciences of the artificial.* Cambridge, MA: The MIT Press, p. 53.
7. *Simon, H.A. (2019). The sciences of the artificial. Cambridge,* MA*: The* MIT *Press*, p. 2.
8. Taylor, G.D. (2014). *When the machine made art: The troubled history of computer art.* London, UK: Bloomsbury.
9. Boden, M.A. (2004). *The creative mind: Myths and mechanisms.* London, UK: Routledge.
10. Alpaydin, E. (2020). *Introduction to machine learning.* Cambridge, MA: The MIT Press.
11. Taylor, G.D. (2014). *When the machine made art: The troubled history of computer art.* London, UK: Bloomsbury ; Boden, M.A. (2004). *The creative mind: Myths and mechanisms.* London, UK: Routledge.
12. Patterson, Z. (2015). *Peripheral vision: Bell labs, the S-C 4020, and the origins of computer art.* Cambridge, MA: The MIT Press.
13. Patterson, Z. (2015). *Peripheral vision: Bell labs, the S-C 4020, and the origins of computer art.* Cambridge, MA: The MIT Press.
14. Patterson, Z. (2015). *Peripheral vision: Bell labs, the S-C 4020, and the origins of computer art.* Cambridge, MA: The MIT Press.
15. Noll, A. M. (1967). The digital computer as a creative medium. IEEE Spectrum. Voil. 4, no. 10, October.
16. Mazzone, M., & Elgammal, A. (2019). Art, Creativity, and the Potential of Artificial Intelligence. *Arts*, 8(1): 26. MDPI AG. Retrieved from http://dx.doi.org/10.3390/arts8010026.

17. Taylor, G.D. (2014). *When the machine made art: The troubled history of computer art.* London, UK: Bloomsbury.

18. Frank, P. (2020). *Sharing code: Art1, Frederick Hammersley, and the dawn of computer art.* Santa Fe: NM: Museum of New Mexico Press.

19. Kepes, G. (ed.) (1956). *The new landscape in art and science.* Chicago, IL: Paul Theobald and Co.

20. Blakinger, J.R. (2019). *Undreaming the Bauhaus.* Cambridge, MA: The MIT Press, p. 7.

21. Blakinger, J.R. (2019). *Undreaming the Bauhaus.* Cambridge, MA: The MIT Press.

22. Blakinger, J.R. (2019). *Undreaming the Bauhaus.* Cambridge, MA: The MIT Press.

23. Gristwood, S., & Kawano, H. (2019). Japan's pioneer of computer arts. *Leonardo,* 52(1): 75–80. doi: https://doi.org/10.1162/leon_a_01605.

24. Taylor, G.D. (2014). *When the machine made art: The troubled history of computer art.* London, UK: Bloomsbury.

25. Leonardo/International Society for the Arts, Sciences, and Technology (ISAST): www.leonardo.info/.

26. Brodsky, J.K. (2002). *Dismantling the patriarchy, bit by bit: Art, feminism, and digital technology.* London, UK: Bloomsbury Visual Arts.

27. Audry, S. (2021). *Art in the age of machine learning.* Cambridge, MA: MIT Press, p. 10 ; Example: https://cloud.google.com/blog/topics/developers-practitioners/baking-recipes-made-ai.

28. Alpaydin, E. (2020). *Introduction to machine learning.* Cambridge, MA: The MIT Press, p. 13.

29. Alpaydin, E. (2020). *Introduction to machine learning.* Cambridge, MA: The MIT Press.

30. Audry, S. (2021). *Art in the age of machine learning.* Cambridge, MA: MIT Press, p. 71.

31. Audry, S. (2021). *Art in the age of machine learning.* Cambridge, MA: MIT Press.

32. Taylor, G.D. (2014). *When the machine made art: The troubled history of computer art.* London, UK: Bloomsbury.

33. Audry, S. (2021). *Art in the age of machine learning.* Cambridge, MA: MIT Press.

34. Audry, S. (2021). *Art in the age of machine learning.* Cambridge, MA: MIT Press.

35. Alpaydin, E. (2020). *Introduction to machine learning.* Cambridge, MA: The MIT Press.

36. Audry, S. (2021). *Art in the age of machine learning.* Cambridge, MA: MIT Press, p. 114.

37. Zhang, K., & Yu, J. (2016). Generation of Kandinsky art. *Leonardo,* 49(1): 48–54. doi: https://doi.org/10.1162/LEON_a_00908.

38. Mazzone, M., & Elgammal, A. (2019). Art, creativity, and the potential of artificial intelligence. *Arts*, 8(1): 26. MDPI AG. Retrieved from http://dx.doi.org/10.3390/arts8010026.

39. Alpaydin, E. (2020). *Introduction to machine learning*. Cambridge, MA: The MIT Press ; Mazzone, M., & Elgammal, A. (2019). Art, creativity, and the potential of artificial intelligence. *Arts*, 8(1): 26. MDPI AG. Retrieved from http://dx.doi.org/10.3390/arts8010026.

40. Goodfellow, I., Pouget-Abadie, J., Mirza, M., Xu, B., Warde-Farley, D., Ozair, S., . . . & Bengio, Y. (2020). Generative adversarial networks. *Communications of the ACM*, 63(11): 139–144.

41. Mazzone, M., & Elgammal, A. (2019). Art, creativity, and the potential of artificial intelligence. *Arts*, 8(1): 26. MDPI AG. Retrieved from http://dx.doi.org/10.3390/arts8010026.

42. Martindale, C. (1990). *The clockwork muse: The predictability of artistic change*. New York: Basic Books.

43. Martindale, *The clockwork muse*, p. 10.

44. Elgammal, A., Liu, B., Elhoseiny, M., & Mazzone, M. (2017). Can: Creative adversarial networks, generating "art" by learning about styles and deviating from style norms. arXiv preprint arXiv:1706.07068.

45. Mazzone, M., & Elgammal, A. (2019). Art, creativity, and the potential of artificial intelligence. *Arts*, 8(1), 26. MDPI AG. Retrieved from http://dx.doi.org/10.3390/arts8010026.

46. Mazzone, M., & Elgammal, A. (2019). Art, creativity, and the potential of artificial intelligence. *Arts*, 8(1): 26. MDPI AG. Retrieved from http://dx.doi.org/10.3390/arts8010026.

47. Elgammal, A., Liu, B., Elhoseiny, M., & Mazzone, M. (2017). Can: Creative adversarial networks, generating "art" by learning about styles and deviating from style norms. arXiv preprint arXiv:1706.07068.

48. Miller, A.I. (2019). *The artist in the machine: The world of AI-powered creativity*. Cambridge, MA: MIT Press.

49. Ashley, K. (2022). *The art of prompts for artificial intelligence: Make art with DALL-E, Midjourney and Livebook AI (Awesome AI)*. Independently Published.

50. https://makeavideo.studio/?fbclid=IwAR1XEoXknIT6NAdA30it2IfJBaCgizcS5V3v5HeBV7gzt6QvBDhJ83nnnpk.

51. https://livebookai.com/post/about.

52. Ashley, K. (2022). *The art of prompts for artificial intelligence: Make art with DALL-E, Midjourney and Livebook AI (Awesome AI)*. Independently Published, p. 57.

53. Steele, J. (2002). *Architecture and computers*. New York: Watson-Guptill Publications.

54. McCarren, F. (2003). *Dancing machines: Choreographies of the age of mechanical reproduction*. Stanford, CA: Sanford University Press.

55. McCarren, F. (2003). *Dancing machines: Choreographies of the age of mechanical reproduction*. Stanford, CA: Sanford University Press, p. 12.

56. McCarren, F. (2003). *Dancing machines: Choreographies of the age of mechanical reproduction*. Stanford, CA: Sanford University Press, p. 102.

57. McCarren, F. (2003). *Dancing machines: Choreographies of the age of mechanical reproduction*. Stanford, CA: Sanford University Press, p. 9.

58. Nakayasu, A. (2020). Animated robotic sculptures: Using SMA motion display to create lifelike movements. *Leonardo*, 53(4): 419–423. doi: https://doi.org/10.1162/leon_a_01929.

59. https://www.youtube.com/watch?v=DeJALYOn940&ab_channel=CarlUnander-Scharin.

60. Unander-Scharin, A., & Unander-Scharin, C. (2016). Robocygne: Dancing Life into an animal-human-machine. *Leonardo*, 49(3): 212–219. doi: https://doi.org/10.1162/LEON_a_01021.

61. Brooks, R. A. (2002) *Flesh and machines: How robots will change us*. New York: Pantheon Books.

62. Bonabeau, E., Dorigo, M., Theraulaz, G. (1999) *Swarm intelligence*. Oxford, UK: Oxford University Press.

63. Greenfield, G. (2014). Penousal Machado; Swarm Art. *Leonardo*, 47(1): 5–7. doi: https://doi.org/10.1162/LEON_a_00695.

64. Moura, L. (2018). Robot Art: An Interview with Leonel Moura. *Arts*, 7(3): 28–. https://doi.org/10.3390/arts7030028.

65. Audry, S., & Ippolito, J. (2019). Can artificial intelligence make art without artists? ask the viewer. *Arts*, 8(1). doi:https://doi.org/10.3390/arts8010035.

66. Clarke, M., Dufeu, F., & Manning, P. (2020). *Inside computer music*. Oxford, UK: Oxford University Press, p. 349.

67. https://sites.google.com/site/deepbachexamples/.

68. Hadjeres, G., Pachet, F., & Nielson, F. (2017). DeepBach: A steerable model for Bach Chorales generation. Proceedings of the 34th International Conference on Machine Learning, PMLR 70: 1362–1371.

69. Miller, A.I. (2019). *The artist in the machine: The world of AI-powered creativity*. Cambridge, MA: MIT Press.

70. Miller, A.I. (2019). *The artist in the machine: The world of AI-powered creativity*. Cambridge, MA: MIT Press.

71. Boden, M.A. (2004). *The creative mind: Myths and mechanisms*. London, UK: Routledge. Ashley, K. (2022). *The art of prompts for artificial intelligence: Make art with DALL-E, Midjourney and Livebook AI (Awesome AI)*. Independently Published.

72. Miller, A.I. (2019). *The artist in the machine: The world of AI-powered creativity*. Cambridge, MA: MIT Press.

73. https://nymag.com/intelligencer/2022/12/chatgpt-wrote-a-pretty-decent-article-about-trump-and-horses.html.

74. Noy, S., & Zhang, W. (2023). Experimental evidence on the productivity effects of generative artificial intelligence. Unpublished MIT paper. https://economics.mit.edu/sites/default/files/inline-files/Noy_Zhang_1.pdf.

75. ChatCBT generated response February 24, 2023.

76. Dixon, S. (2007). *Digital performance: A history of new media in theater, dance, performance art, and installation*. Cambridge, MA: The MIT Press.

77. Dixon, S. (2007). *Digital performance: A history of new media in theater, dance, performance art, and installation.* Cambridge, MA: The MIT Press, p. 47.
78. Dixon, S. (2007). *Digital performance: A history of new media in theater, dance, performance art, and installation.* Cambridge, MA: The MIT Press.
79. Jessop, E. (2015). Capturing the Body Live: A Framework for Technological Recognition and Extension of Physical Expression in Performance. *Leonardo*, 48(1): 32–38. doi: https://doi.org/10.1162/LEON_a_00935.
80. Dixon, S. (2007). *Digital performance: A history of new media in theater, dance, performance art, and installation.* Cambridge, MA: The MIT Press.
81. https://sites.utexas.edu/theatredance-blog/2018/03/02/inside-look-the-life-and-career-of-dr-yacov-sharir/.
82. https://waynemcgregor.com/.
83. Leach, J., & deLahunta, S. (2017). Dance becoming knowledge: Designing a digital "body." *Leonardo*, 50(5): 461–467. doi: https://doi.org/10.1162/LEON_a_01074 ; McCormick, J., Hossny, M., Fielding, M., Mullins, J., Vincent, J.B., Hossny, M., Vincs, K., Mohamed, S., Nahavandi, S., Creighton, D. & Hutchison, S. (2020). Feels like dancing: Motion capture-driven haptic interface as an added sensory experience for dance viewing. *Leonardo*, 53(1): 45–49. doi: https://doi.org/10.1162/leon_a_01689.
84. Johnston, A. (2015). Conversational interaction in interactive dance works. *Leonardo*, 48(3): 296–297. doi: https://doi.org/10.1162/LEON_a_01017.
85. Brett. (2020). Libby Heaney bridges the gap between science and art. A former quantum scientist she is now a full-time artist. Quantum Zeitgeist, October 19. https://quantumzeitgeist.com/libby-heaney-bridges-the-gap-between-science-and-art-a-former-quantum-scientist-she-is-now-a-full-time-artist/.
86. Johung, J. (2015). Choreographic Arrhythmias. *Leonardo*, 48(2): 172–173. doi: https://doi.org/10.1162/LEON_a_00975.
87. Mitchell, T., Hyde, J., Tew, P., & Glowacki, D.R. (2016). Danceroom spectroscopy: At the frontiers of physics, performance, interactive art and technology. *Leonardo*, 49(2): 138–147. doi: https://doi.org/10.1162/LEON_a_00924 ; https://pubs.rsc.org/en/content/articlehtml/2014/fd/c4fd00008k ; https://www.danceroom-spec.com/.
88. Glowacki, D., Tew, P., Hyde, J., Kriefman, L., Mitchell, T., Price, J., & McIntosh-Smith, S. (2013). Using human energy fields to sculpt real-time molecular dynamics. In L. Fruk, & P. Weibel (Eds.), *Molecular aesthetics.* Cambridge, MA: MIT Press.
89. Dixon, S. (2007). *Digital performance: A history of new media in theater, dance, performance art, and installation.* Cambridge, MA: The MIT Press.
90. Turing, A.M. (1950). Computing machinery and intelligence. Mind. Volume LIX, Issue 236, October 1950, Pages 433–460, https://doi.org/10.1093/mind/LIX.236.433.
91. Michie, D. (1968). Computer—servant or master. *Spectrum.* No. 45.
92. Chalmers, D.J. (2010). *The character of consciousness.* Oxford, UK: Oxford University Press.

93. Gleiser, M. (2022). *Great minds don't think alike: Debates on Consciousness, reality, intelligence, faith, time, AI, immortality, and the human.* New York: Columbia University Press.

94. Dehaene, S. (2014). *Consciousness and the brain: Deciphering how the brain codes our thoughts.* New York: Penguin.

95. Graziano, M.S.A. (2019). *Rethinking consciousness: A scientific theory of subjective experience.* New York: W.W. Norton & Company.

96. Skrbina, D. (2005). *Panpsychism in the West.* Cambridge, MA: The MIT Press.

97. Dehaene, S. (2014). *Consciousness and the brain: Deciphering how the brain codes our thoughts.* New York: Penguin.

98. Elgammal, A., Liu, B., Elhoseiny, M., & Mazzone, M. (2017). Can: Creative adversarial networks, generating "art" by learning about styles and deviating from style norms. arXiv preprint arXiv:1706.07068.

99. https://www.moma.org/calendar/exhibitions/5535.

Chapter 5

Biological Art

As seen in the first two chapters in reviewing the history of aesthetics, many philosophers point to nature as a model of beauty, either to appreciate or to imitate. Yet for most of these same scholars, the notion that the natural world, not just humans, creates art would seem preposterous. Nevertheless, by the middle of the 20th century, artists began to challenge the humancentric notion of art. There were two major fronts where this occurred: in the machine and computer learning area described in the previous chapter, and in the world of living organisms.

The work of artists interacting with nature comprises a wide range of activities from the incorporation of natural materials and images into artworks, the simple genetic manipulation of plants, to modifying living organisms for artistic purposes. At its simplest form, bio art is the appreciation of the beauty of nature seen through powerful microscopes and telescopes. The earliest examples of bio art involve plant breeding. The latest bio art uses startling genetic editing tools to manipulate living organisms.

Some argue that bio art is a new imaginative form, one created in test tubes and laboratories instead of art studios. As with computer science, biotechnology is likely to enter popular culture and be used in cultural, not just scientific, ways.[1] Furthermore, while scientists generally tend to strongly resist any effort to claim that animals make art, some point to the success of such efforts with highly intelligent animals, such as elephants and chimpanzees.

At the beginning of the 21st century, the rise of biotechnology and the rapid advancement of human understanding of DNA led to a revolution in what is variously known as biological art, bio art, life art, or living art. In general, these permutations link artistic practice with scientific practices using living matter for artistic ends. Figure 5.1 is a graphic representation of the overlap and distinctions among various terms used in the evolving field of bio art.

According to the artist Eduardo Kac, bio art manipulates the processes of life, employing approaches that include the coaching of biological materials

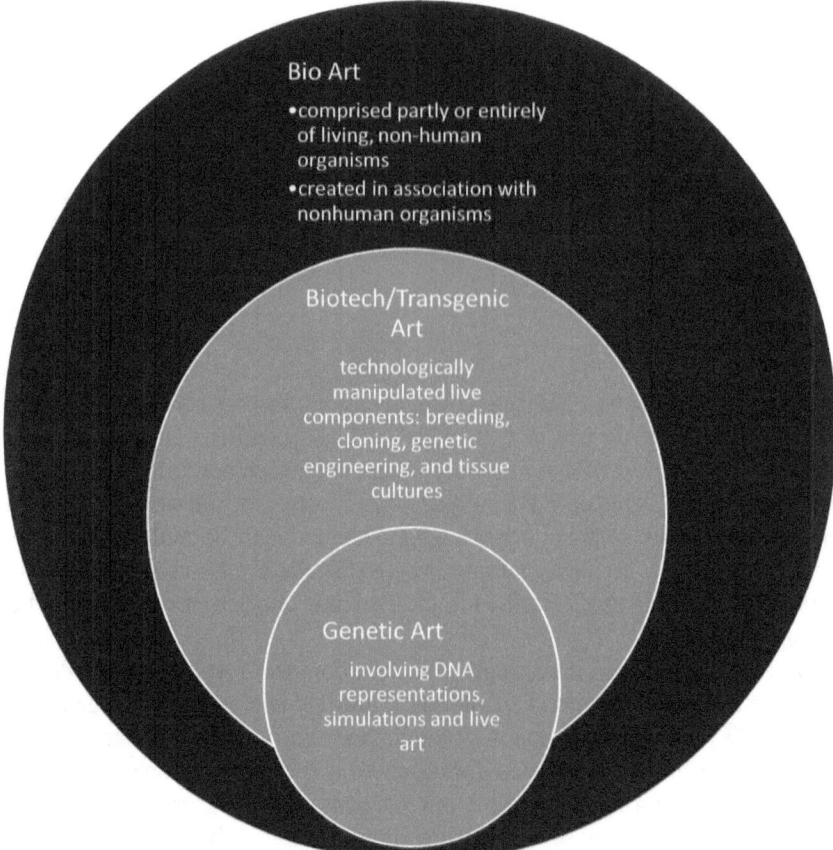

Figure 5.1. Bio Art Terminology. Based on Gessert, 2010, "Appendix II," from Pier Luigi Capucci in Hauser, J., Capucci, P.L. & Torriano, F. (2007). *Art Biotech*. Bologna, Italy: CLUEB.

into shapes and movements, the use of biotech tools, and the transformation of living organisms without integration.[2]

> It is in this organic sense that bio art uses the properties of life and its materials, changes organisms within their own species, or invents life with new characteristics. Bio art stakes evolutionary strategies that offer alternatives to mainstream notions of beauty.[3]

Kac distinguishes bio art from digital media that depicts biological themes and images. Scholars also separate bio art used as striking pictures versus a more thoughtful context. Bio art is at times employed to provoke ethical and political discussions about the field of biotechnology.

Bio art challenges the anthropocentrism that tends to dominate conceptions of what art is and can lead to new ways of thinking.

> Living things can remind us that nonhuman forms of life are not simply raw materials but entities that do not need us for validation or improvement. Bio art presents a window of opportunity for producing new kinds of consciousness.[4]

Biocybernetics is yet another term used in the field. Scholars identify some of the theoretical premises of "biocybernetic" art objects. In much of biocybernetic art, beauty emerges in the form of adaptive mechanisms, such as in robotic tetrapods or in self-organizing artificial plants. Nam June Paik, Edward Ihnawitz, Ulrike Gabriel, and Gilberto Esparza are leading biocybernetic artists.[5]

Bio art employs a range of organisms, including bacteria, fungi, and slime molds.[6] Specializations within the area include bio-ecological art and biotech art involving technological manipulation. In the late 20th century, conceptual artists such as Jannis Kounellis, Joseph Beuys, and Hans Haacke explored using living materials in an interactive manner. For instance, Haacke produced works using live grass, chickens, ants, seagulls, turtles, goldfish, goats and myna birds.[7] In Table 5.1 the range of organisms used in bio art is displayed. One can see there has been great variety in approaches by artists over an extensive period.

Carrie Rohman, in *Choreographies of the Living: Bioaesthetics in Literature, Art, and Performance*, contends that human creativity is only the most recent iteration of an artistic impulse that belongs to the living in general. Aesthetics from this perspective must be understood as bioaesthetics.[8]

> Rather than looking primarily "beyond" ourselves to understand animals and aesthetics, I suggest we must also look "within" to identify a deep coincidence of the human and animal elaboration of life forces in aesthetic practices. Moreover, we ought to turn toward animals to revise and revivify our understanding of human aesthetic capacities.[9]

Rohman claims there is a strong link between bioaesthetics and modern art: "Modernism is itself a kind of aesthetic 'becoming-other,' and thus the bioaesthetic is especially prominent in this period."[10]

In this chapter, we consider the development of the field of biological art. Both philosophical and ethical questions that arise from this surprising aesthetic field are outlined.

Table 5.1 Organisms in Bio Art

Organism	Artists	Artwork	Date
amoebae	Eduardo Kac	The Eighth Day	2000-2001
ants	Hans Haacke	Ant-Cooperative	1969
bacteria	Peter Gerwin Hoffmann	Mikroben bei Kandinsky	1988
Bamboo	Marta de Menezes	Nature?	1999
Butterflies	Damien Hirst	In and Out of Love	1991
Cats	Dave Powell	ArtCats	2010
Cells, human	Paul Perry	Good and Evil on the Long Voyage	1997
Elephants	Braco Dimitrijevic	When Elephants Were Reheating . . .	1983
Fungi	Philip Ross	Chunky	1999
Goat	Hans Haacke	Goats in a Forest. Grazing	1970
Grasshoppers	Huang Yong Ping	Theatre of the World—Bridge	1993
Green algae	Zbigniew Oksiuta	Breed Areas	2004
Moss	Jun Takita	Light Only Light	2004
Rats (transgenic)	Kathy High	Embracing Animal	2006
Tadpoles (transgenic)	Dmitry Bulatov	Senses Alert	2000
Tarantulas	Huang Yong Ping	Theatre of the World—Bridge	1993
Watercress	Ken Rinaldo & Amy Youngs	Farm Fountain	2008
Yeast (transgenic)	Critical Art Ensemble	The Cult of the New Eve	1999

Source: Based on Gessert, 2010

USING TECHNOLOGY TO UNCOVER BEAUTY UP CLOSE AND FAR AWAY

Since the advent of synthetic organic chemistry in the mid-19th century, chemists have frequently pointed to the creativity, imagination, and aesthetic inspiration required for chemical synthesis. "The fact that technology allows us to transcend the limits of natural perception and see what was previously 'unseeable' creates the new dimension of aesthetic experience and practice we call 'molecular aesthetics.'"[11]

Abstract art has been inspired by biological and molecular images, as seen in specific artists, designers, and architects, including Richard Buckminster Fuller, Rudolf Arnheim, Charles Eames, and György Kepes. The ecological art movement of the 1960s and 1970s employed microorganisms and real

Biological Art

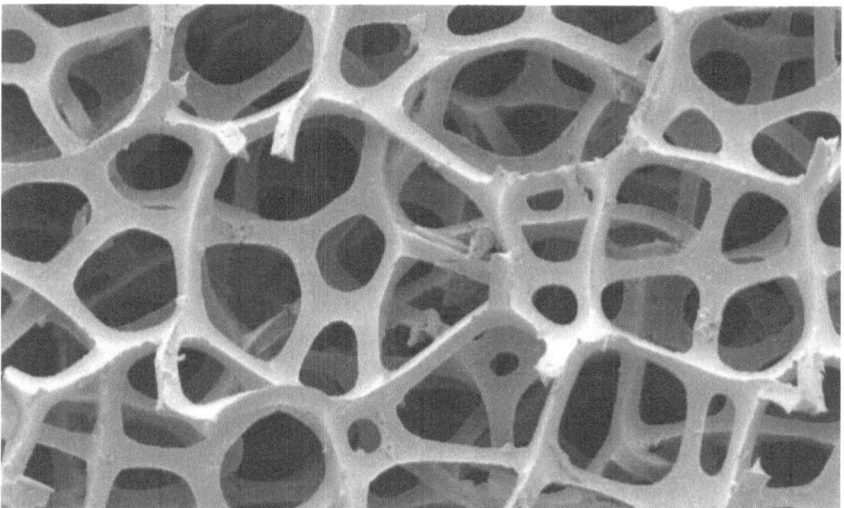

Figure 5.2. Fibrous Configuration of a Dry Macrofoam Sponge Swab. CDC, Janice Haney Carr, 2007

natural restoration projects, such as Sonfist's *Time Landscape: Greenwich Village, New York* in 1978.

The previous chapter discussed György Kepes and the important work he did at MIT in leading the art and science collaboration. One of his legacies was editing a book series called *Vision and Value* concentrating on various issues linked to the exploration of science and art. Based on the MIT exhibit he curated in 1951, *The New Landscape Exhibition*, he published a subsequent book of the same name. Naum Gabo, in a chapter in that book on *Art and Science*, writes:

> Now the sciences have enabled us to grow supplementary organs to our five senses in the form of new multiple and complicated devices; we behold an entirely new image of these mysterious forces. The effect of these discoveries on the scientist's mind, as of all other discoveries, is straightforward and pragmatic. He steps into these new vistas as a conqueror, making use of all he finds there to benefit human life and to better our orientation in this world of ours. But what are the consequences to the modern artist of the new horizons opened by the scientists? The artist of to-day cannot possibly escape the impact science is making on the whole mentality of the human race.[12]

Gabo explains one kind of new art that Kepes can display in stunning fashion in his book series showing pictures of microorganisms, tissues, and crystals that the public had not generally seen before. Furthermore, using the increasingly powerful telescopic and satellite images, it can show the world from a great distance. Figure 5.3 is a contemporary example of a NASA image seen from a billion kilometers away, through the ice and dust particles of Saturn's rings. Earth appears as a tiny, bright dot and emphasizes man's position in the vast physical universe.

Charles Morris, in his chapter in the same volume on *Man-Cosmos Symbols*, comments:

> An old Buddhist technique was to imagine oneself as small as an insect, and to view things from this perspective; and then immediately to become in imagination as large as a mountain and to survey insect and man from this perspective. The photographs in this book facilitate such exercises. They permit us, symbolically, to juxtapose the most diverse orders and dimensions of the cosmos, to look from below and above, to be inside and outside simultaneously. They can minister in this way to the strange but deep need of man to be great while being small and to remain small while becoming great.[13]

Walter Gropius, the well-known German architect and Bauhaus to America transplant, in his article *Reorientation*, contends that in nature, utility and beauty are interdependent: "Is the maker of the rose or the tulip an artist or a technician? Both, for in nature utility and beauty are constitutional qualities, mutually and truthfully interdependent."[14]

Figure 5.3. A View of Earth from Saturn. NASA, Cassini, Image courtesy CICLOPS team, January 16, 2007

In another 1965 Kepes-edited volume, *Structure in Art and in Science*, C.S. Smith writes succinctly about the powerful new images of nature that technology provided:

> Anyone who works with the microscope for an intellectual or practical purpose will frequently pause for a moment of sheer enjoyment of the patterns that he sees, for they have much in common with formal art.[15]

Smith claims there is a close analogy between a work of the dimensions in human artwork and the structure of a piece of metal or rock resulting from interactions between the atoms and electrons composing it.

Bronowski, in his chapter on *The Discovery of Form*, comments that while the public at the time was largely unaware of the great changes in science, artists were sensitive to the transformation and reflected it in their work. He asserts that abstract painting and modern sculpture especially reveal the shifts.[16] He summarizes the differences this way:

> For fifty years we have been living in an intellectual revolution, in which interest has shifted from the surface appearance to the underlying structure, and then from the gross structure to the fine organization of minute parts in which only the total pattern expresses an order.[17]

Finally, in the same volume in the series, Buckminster Fuller, in *Conceptuality of Fundamental Structures*, contends that a break between science and the public occurred when, with the microscope, previously invisible natural behavior was revealed without the need for conceptual models.

> With the wholesale migration of science into the world of invisibility without any conceptual models of reference, the literary man who depended upon conceptual models or analogies for his verbal pattern relaying was automatically excluded from either ring-side participation or back row glimpsing of the significant affairs of science.[18]

In this way, Fuller points to the ongoing challenge of negotiating the synthesis of art and science.

ANIMAL ART

There are thirty million Google searches per month on the word *cats*. A recent search for the most popular YouTube cat video finds that "Cat ChangAn Makes the World's LARGEST Gummy Bear"—in which a chef cat on a cooking show makes Gummy Bears—was viewed 304 million times.[19] Second only to pornography, photographs, videos, and graphics of cats fill the internet. Why?

This is the question scholar Jody Berland asks in her book *Virtual Menageries: Animals as Mediators in Network Cultures*. She claims that animal representations are employed throughout history to change social configurations. Evolving human visual capacities and technologies employed images of animals to soften reactions: "These configurations are part of what makes us human—not because we are different from them but because they are an essential part of everything we are and do."[20]

Animals have been conscripted as sacrifices, symbols, and items of trade. With the exchange of animals in new social encounters, humans sought to initiate connections and to occupy other technologies and communication spaces. For example, animals appeared in the first demonstrations of early film and digital media. From *Boxing Cats*, an early Thomas Edison film made in 1894, to Felix the Cat, Mickey Mouse, and Pluto the Dog, early film and animation is filled with animal images.[21]

Berland argues that human encounters with animals in various forms call attention to our existential experience of embodied life. As humans evolve rapidly in the use of new technologies, animals play an important mediating role. Although the images may appear cute and superficial, they are popular because they strike deep: "We deny our humanity when we deny our deep connections with these animals."[22]

One survey about what people prefer to see in paintings of landscapes found a preference for animals in natural settings, and outdoor scenes over interiors. It is plausible that we are genetically disposed to respond aesthetically to animals, either positively or negatively, because in the distant past, such responses were adaptive in that they guided the judgments of successful ancestors who survived. Humans admire features in animals that are appealing in humans, such as fitness and grace.

> We admire animals' aesthetic character as a result of viewing them literally as God's artworks or imaginatively as pseudo-artworks. We abstract their appearances from their natural context in order to engage aesthetically with these as formal, expressive, or sensory arrays.[23]

Darwin thought that birds, mammals, and even insects possess aesthetic taste. Regarding the question of animals as artists, Davies argues that humpback whales would be the most plausible candidate because of their complex songs, which are hierarchically ordered. Members of the same whale population sing the same song, but this continuously and rapidly evolves and changes in a seemingly improvisational manner.[24]

In 1910, Roland Dorgeles on a lark submitted three works painted by a donkey with a brush tied to its tail to the Salon des Independents in Paris. Lolo, the donkey, belonged to the proprietor of the Lapin Agile in Montmartre, where Picasso and his friends often gathered. One painted with the donkey tail technique reportedly sold for the equivalent of over 1,200 Euros.[25]

The perception of animals as art makers has come a long way since the late 1950s, when the celebrated ethologist and amateur painter Desmond Morris curated an exhibition of chimpanzee art at the Institute of Contemporary Arts (ICA) in London. Included in the show were works by Congo, a frequent and popular guest on Morris's television program *Zootime*. According to studies, chimpanzees exhibit artistic development over time—Congo's pictures were said to become increasingly complex. Even Picasso was said to have owned a painting by Congo.[26]

Animals are progressively viewed not so much as novelties, but as sophisticated creators with skills and senses that can enhance projects in ways humans never can. It has become commonplace for zoos and even aquariums to offer art supplies to a wide variety of species, part of enrichment efforts to keep animals physically and mentally stimulated. The projects are designed to tap into natural behaviors so that sloth bears who feed by blowing away dirt on the forest floor and sucking up termites are given a straw-like apparatus to blow paint onto a canvas, and frogs receive a paint-like substance created from the powdered algae mix they typically use as food.[27]

Since the mid-1950s, zoos have used art activity for animals and have sold their products in fund-raising efforts.[28] In 2012, London's Grant Museum of

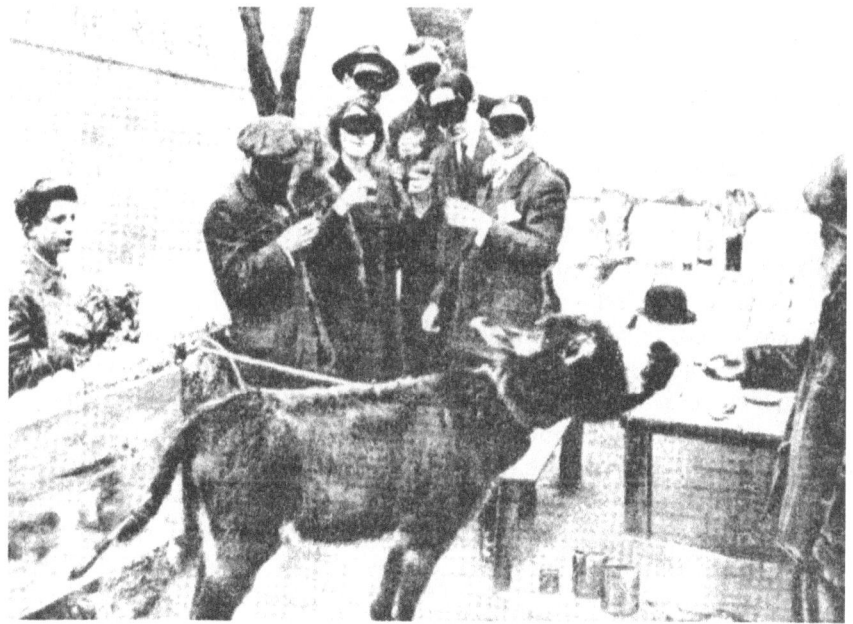

Figure 5.4.   Lolo and the Pranksters 1910. Unknown

Zoology staged what organizers claimed was the first interspecies show of paintings by animals. A highlight of the exhibition was a painting of a flowerpot by the elephant named Boon Mee, formerly a logging elephant from Thailand. *The Art by Animals* show features art by elephants, orangutans, gorillas, and chimps.

In terms of specific performing arts, Isadora Duncan's animal engagements are central to the fundamental gestures of modern dance.

> The way Duncan revolutionized dance must be recognized as embracing the vibrating animality of the human body and of human experience: in this sense modern dance in the twentieth century represents the eruption of the animal into Western dance practice.[29]

In this way, "animality" is at the center of aesthetic expression in much of contemporary art forms.

In June 2010, Laurie Anderson and her husband, Lou Reed, created a symphony called *Music for Dogs* that was written for an audience of dogs. The premise was that dogs can hear sounds inaudible to humans and have different preferences in music. This challenges the anthropocentric presumption that art is only for homo sapiens.[30]

Bush and Silver, in their satirical *Why Cats Paint: A Theory of Feline Aesthetics*, cover the world of cats reportedly painting, exhibiting, and selling their work. Evidently, cats paint only in acrylic because oils smell remarkably like their own urine. Scientists theorize that cat painting may be motivated by territorial marking behavior. Some dismiss it as a merely vertical marking activity, not a creative expression.[31]

The authors in a witty manner profile a fictional group of successful international cat artists, including "Bootsie" from San Francisco, who, in five painting exhibits, earned more than seventy-five thousand dollars and the Zampa d'Oro (Golden Paw) award at the Exposizione dell'Arte Felino in Milan in 1993. Bootsie's method is described:

> As soon as the easel is put up on the lawn and the paints are laid out next to it, any hint of feline disdain, any trace of detached hauteur, vanishes completely. He almost pounces on the paint as if he must trap its fleeting vibrance before it escapes, and the moment it is on his paw he springs up to apply it.[32]

In another fictional profile from the book, "Minnie," who lives in a little vineyard in Aix-en-Provence, paints in an abstract expressionist style with paintings fetching an average of ten thousand dollars each. One reviewer from an exhibit in Arles claimed that "her many colors and directions allow us to glimpse the inner feline reality."[33]

DEVELOPMENT OF BIO ART

The evolution of bio art has a long and exceptionally varied history. In his 1936 show at the Museum of Modern Art in New York, the photographer Edward Steichen was the first artist to create new organisms to exhibit in a major museum. His hybridized delphiniums were raised by hand and manipulated with chemicals for effect. Steichen's show was covered by forty-two newspapers and caused a great deal of discussion about what was appropriate for display in a museum show. Exhibiting living matter raised questions about originality and aesthetics. Steichen argued that such manipulation of nature was a creative art. His genetic art can still be purchased online in seed form.[34]

By the end of the 19th century, many influential thinkers argued that garden plants were art. The first book about plants as fine art was Sacheverell Sitwell's *Old Fashioned Flowers*, contending that ornamental plants "represent a direct and conscious attack upon Nature." The first artist to treat plant breeding as a fine art is often listed as photographer Edward Steichen, who began breeding plants while living outside Paris in the early 20th century.

Figure 5.5. Installation View of the Exhibition, *Edward Steichen's Delphiniums*. The Museum of Modern Art, New York. June 24, 1936 through July 1, 1936. Photograph by Edward Steichen. Digital Image © The Museum of Modern Art/Licensed by SCALA / Art Resource, NY. Artist: Steichen, Edward (1879–1973) © ARS, NY

However, Steichen's 1936 show at MOMA, described earlier, was unique and not followed by similar shows at other museums.[35]

Two years after the MOMA show, Salvador Dali's *Rainy Taxi* installation at the 1938 International Exposition of Surrealism in Paris featured female mannequins surrounded by lettuce covered by feeding Burgundian snails.

Beyond whole animal organisms, artists use human body tissue, urine, and blood to create works. The use of bodily fluids has a long tradition in the 20th century from Marcel Duchamp's 1946 sperm drawing entitled *Faulty Landscape*, blood and urine used in the *Vienna Actionism* movement, and Andy Warhol's 1978 series of *piss paintings* produced through the reaction of copper metallic painting and urine.

In 1991, Mark Quinn created *Self*, a model of his head containing nine liters of his own frozen blood featured in a Brooklyn Museum of Art exhibition. In 2001, he used DNA to make *A Genomic Portrait: Sir John Sulston*, a work in which the sitter's genetic material was used to create an abstract image. Quinn created the portrait of the Nobel Prize winner using standard DNA cloning methods, which was then unveiled at London's National Portrait Gallery.[36]

The Algae Society BioArt Design Lab is a global interdisciplinary collective of artists, scientists, and scholars experimenting with algae seeking to highlight complex human interdependence and kinship. They endeavor to shift our perspectives from humancentric exceptionalism to greater appreciation and cultural reframing of our responsibility as participants in "multispecies worlding."[37]

Stunning images of algae have been presented in several shows. For example, Confluence at the Cameron Art Museum, in Wilmington, North Carolina, was said by one reviewer to decenter the human:

> The repositioning of the human has irrevocably impacted, for the better, the ways that we produce knowledge through art. Exhibitions such as are a great example of how posthumanist philosophies can radically reshape both the form and the content of contemporary art.[38]

Jennifer Parker's Algae Digital Kaleidoscope & Tapestry combines scanned images of seaweed with diagrams of diatoms to create a meditative tapestry and kaleidoscope fashioned for contemporary contemplation with music by Liron Studios, in Parque Leloir, Buenos Aires, Argentina.[39]

Parker is an artist and professor of Art and Digital Art & New Media and founding director of the OpenLab Collaborative Research Center at the University of California, Santa Cruz.[40] As with many biological artists and scientists, her work and research discusses ethical dimensions of the linkage between science and art.[41]

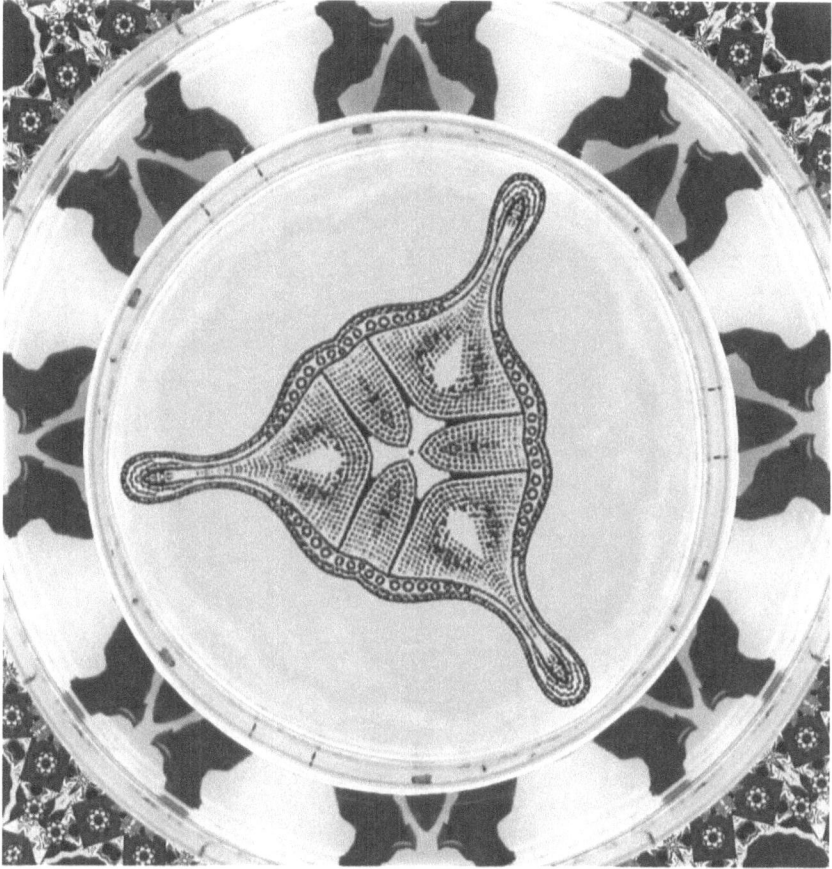

Figure 5.6. Algae Digital Kaleidoscope & Tapestry. Jennifer Parker, 2022, image still #4

Attracted to Light by Geoffrey Mann narrates the erratic behavior of a moth upon the stimulus of light. The insect's path through the air is captured using cinematic technology and materialized through rapid prototyping, or 3D printing. The design is part of Mann's Long Exposure series, which also features lamps based on the trajectories of a bird in flight, taking off, and landing.

HUMANS INTERACTING WITH LIVING ORGANISMS

Starting with small organisms, artists have been inspired by proteins re-creating the first step of the emergence of three-dimensional bodies from one-dimensional DNA inspiring a more holistic view of nature.[42] For

Figure 5.7. *Attracted to Light*. Artist: Geoffrey Mann, UK, Long Exposure series, SLS nylon, LED, 2005, Image © Sylvain Deleu

instance, Regina Trindade uses protein analysis technique to create flexible and transparent gels that behave like a sieve, creating startling images.[43]

Bacteria is one organism often used by artists. In 1987, the Australian Peter Gerwin Hoffmann exhibited *Mikroben bei Kandinsky*, consisting of cultures of bacteria scraped from the surface of a Kandinsky painting.[44] In 1984, Joe Davis at MIT and Berkeley created *Microvenus*, a segment of DNA inserted into a E.coli bacterium—the first "transgenic artwork" created through genetic engineering.[45]

In his sculptures, drawings, and installations, Mick Lorusso explores the transformations of energy and water in living systems, at the levels of the microbial, the bodily, and the urban. Recently Lorusso created two sculptural

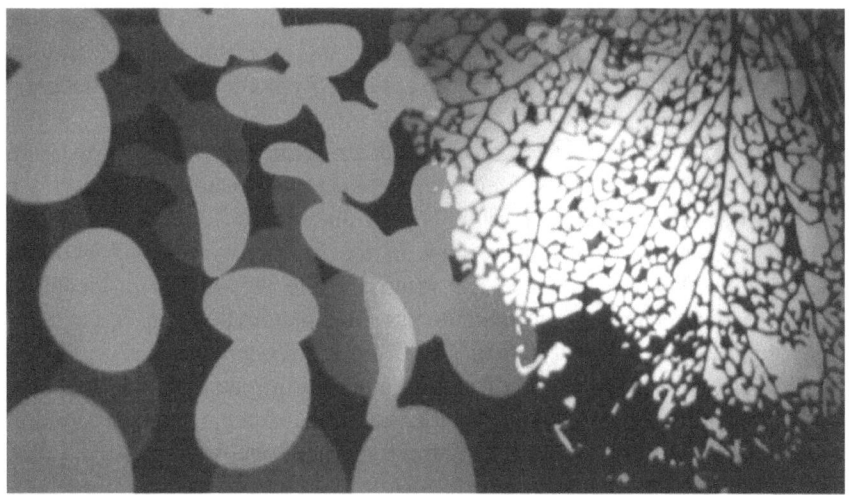

Figure 5.8. *Coherence*. Quantum Biology Series. Mick Lorusso, Shadow performance video still, 2021

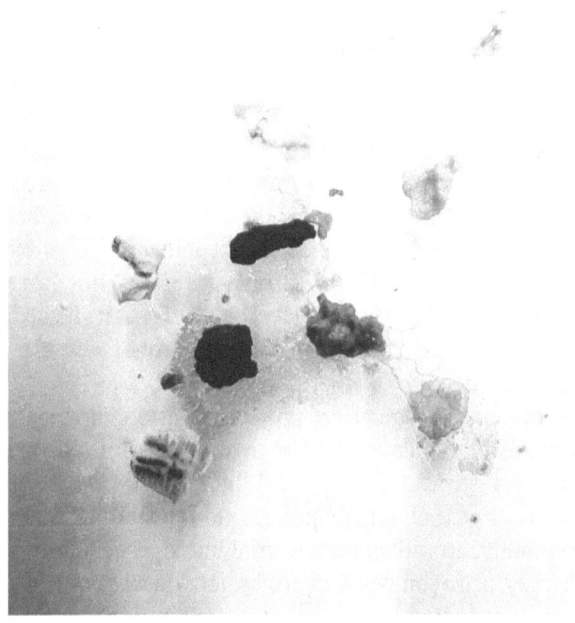

Figure 5.9. Star Diagram. Sarah Grant

projects with bacteria that produce electricity while decomposing organic matter, in a technology known as a microbial fuel cell. Relationships among humans, technology, and microbes are said to emerge in these theatrical scenarios.[46]

Slime mold is another organism popular with bio artists. Artist and engineer Sarah Grant collaborated with architect and researcher Selena Savic on hybrid bio-networking experiments with slime mold.[47]

Insects have also made their mark in the bio art world. Andrea Zittel breeds houseflies in her Brooklyn studio. While an artist-in-residence at MASS MoCA, Natalie Jeremijinko documented pattern diversity in ten thousand ladybugs in a project named *The Great LadyBug Animation*.[48] *Applied Design*, MoMA's 2014 show of cutting-edge design acquisitions, included Tomáš Gabzdil Libertíny's *Made by Bees*, a vase-shaped beehive scaffold in a bee colony. The process took forty thousand bees one week to build a hive around the form.[49]

Dieter Roth invited insects to dine on a chocolate artwork at a MoMA show.[50] The title is a reference to the 1916 novel *A Portrait of the Artist as a Young Man* by James Joyce, but the artwork is a portrait of Roth as an old man, cast in a mixture of chocolate and birdseed. It was intended to be mounted on a post in the open air and consumed by birds until nothing remained.

María Fernanda Cardoso worked with jumping fleas and self-camouflaging katydids.[51] Her past sculptural works have often been inspired by the animal world was interested in raising and training live fleas. When performing *Cardoso Flea Circus*, Cardoso leads her fleas through a series of acrobatic efforts, which include dancing, tightrope walks, high dives, and weightlifting.

Larger organisms are also used for active interaction with artists. Eduardo Kac introduced the term *transgenic art* as art based on genetic engineering to create unique living beings. In his 2000 *GFP Bunny* work, he genetically engineered a rabbit with an added fluorescent jellyfish gene. However, the French laboratory where the rabbit was raised decided not to release it for exhibition. Another example is Garnet Hertz's Cockroach-Controlled Mobile Robot, which allowed a cockroach to control a robot vehicle, integrating insects with high-tech design.[52]

The range of human biological art projects is astounding, including conceptual artist Orlan's manipulation of her own body with plastic surgeries to shape her features as historical and mythical figures.[53] Joe Davis, in his *Poetica Vaginal*, in 1986 attempted an artistic project "to transmit vaginal contractions into space to communicate with extraterrestrial intelligence." It involved artists, engineers, biologists, astronomers, and professional dancers.[54]

Adam Zaretsky's *microinjection works* are explorative works of transgenic production. One such work is *The Brainus*, an anus made of biopolymers seeded with brain tissue.[55] Marion Laval-Jeantet and Benoit Mangin created

Biological Art 129

Figure 5.10. *The Honeycomb Vase "Made by Bees."* 2006. Beeswax, 9 x 5 1/2 x 5 ½" (22.9 x 14 x 14 cm). Manufactured by Studio Libertiny. Gift of The Aaron and Betty Lee Stern Foundation. Digital Image © The Museum of Modern Art/Licensed by SCALA / Art Resource, NY. Artist: Libertiny, Tomas Gabzdil (b. 1979)

Skin Culture in 1997, investigating the fantasy of changing the human body through skin cultures tattooed with images of animals and exhibited in jars of preservative liquid.[56]

Established in 1996 by Oron Catts and Ionat Zurr, the Tissue Culture & Art Project explores how tissue engineering can be used as a medium for artistic

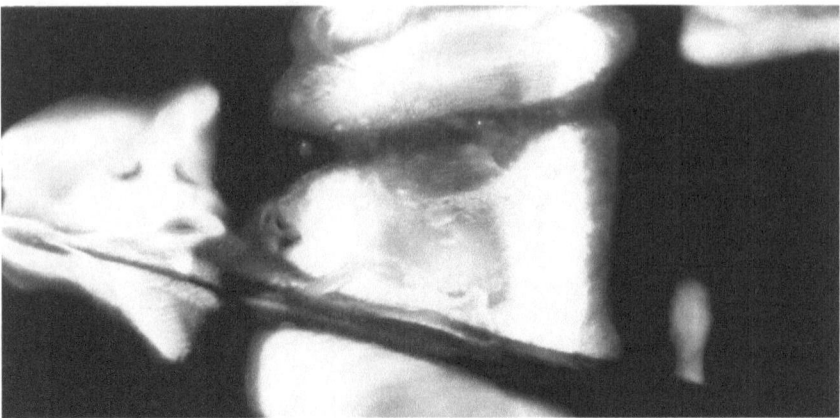

Figure 5.11. Tissue Culture & Art Project. Oron Catts and Ionat Zurr

expression. Their projects have dealt with lab-grown food, tissue-cultured clothing, semi-living sculptures, and the changing relationship between humans and nonhumans.

The image in Figure 5.11 was created by Catts and Zurr in a first stage growing, monitoring, and presenting partially living objects as pieces of art. Fibroblast and epidermal cells grew over three-dimensional, human-made technological artefacts. Three-dimensional computer-animated sequences depicted the growth of the living artefact, which was then documented using medical imaging technologies.

The Tissue Culture & Art Project coined the term *semi-living* to describe cells and tissues that are isolated from organisms and coerced to grow in predetermined shapes. These creations are examples that bring into question common perceptions of life and identity, and the position of humans regarding other living beings and the environment. The primary aim of the TC&A Project is as stated: to explore the philosophical, cultural, and ethical implications of the semi-living and the "contestable futures scenarios they offer us."[57]

CONCLUSION

This chapter delved into the unconventional world of biological art. While for many the idea of computer-created art is challenging, animals making art and humans manipulating living organisms for artistic purposes seems bizarre. For centuries scientists resisted any effort to claim that animals make art, arguing that to do so is a form of anthropomorphism, yet many point to the success of such efforts. Regardless, with both the rise of strong instrumentation to see into microscopic worlds and distant galaxies, along with the biotechnological ability to manipulate living organisms, the hold of humans on creativity is slipping.

Finally, both ethical and philosophical questions arise from this surprising aesthetic field. It is in the manipulation of living things that ethical concerns arise, as seen in work involving the possible inhumane use of animals and living organisms. Nevertheless, for most artists and scientists working in the biological art area, the clear purpose is to celebrate and honor the natural world and living things and raise questions about ethical treatment and sustainability.

Bio art provokes a startling reframing of the world around us, and traditional notions of art. In the conclusion next, the crucial issues arising in this and previous chapters are discussed.

NOTES

1. Kac, E. (2007). *Signs of life: Bio art and beyond.* Cambridge, MA: The MIT Press.

2. Kac, E. (2007). *Signs of life: Bio art and beyond.* Cambridge, MA: The MIT Press.

3. Kac, E. (2007). *Signs of life: Bio art and beyond.* Cambridge, MA: The MIT Press, p. 18.

4. Gessert, G. (2010). *Green light: Toward an art of evolution.* Cambridge, MA: The MIT Press, p. 139.

5. Thompson, R. (2014). Tirtha Prasad Mukhopadhyay; Aesthetics of biocybernetic designs: A systems approach to biorobots and its implications for the environment. *Leonardo*, 47(4): 318–324. doi: https://doi.org/10.1162/LEON_a_00836.

6. Gessert, G. (2010). *Green light: Toward an art of evolution.* Cambridge, MA: The MIT Press.

7. https://en.wikipedia.org/wiki/Hans_Haacke.

8. Rohman, C. (2018). *Choreographies of the living.* Oxford, UK: Oxford University Press.

9. Rohman, C. (2018). *Choreographies of the living.* Oxford, UK: Oxford University Press,, p. 7.

10. Rohman, C. (2018). *Choreographies of the living.* Oxford, UK: Oxford University Press, p. 13.

11. Weibel, P. & Fruk, L. (eds). (2014). *Molecular aesthetics.* Cambridge, MA: The MIT Press, p. 33.

12. Kepes, G. (ed.) (1956). *The new landscape in art and science.* Chicago, IL: Paul Theobald and Co., p. 61.

13. Morris, C. Man-Cosmos Symbols. In Kepes, G. (ed.) (1956), *The new landscape in art and science.* Chicago, IL: Paul Theobald and Co., p. 99.

14. Gropius, W. Reorientation. In Kepes, G. (ed.) (1956), *The new landscape in art and science.* Chicago, IL: Paul Theobald and Co., p. 94.

15. Smith, C.S. Structure substructure superstructure. In Kepes, G. (ed.) (1965), *Structure in art and in science*. New York: George Braziller, p. 29.
16. Bronowski, J. The discovery of form. In Kepes, G. (ed.) (1965), *Structure in art and in science*. New York: George Braziller, p. 60.
17. Bronowski, J. The discovery of form. In Kepes, G. (ed.) (1965), *Structure in art and in science*. New York: George Braziller, p. 60.
18. Fuller, B. Conceptuality of fundamental structures. In Kepes, G. (ed.) (1965), *Structure in art and in science*. New York: George Braziller, p. 80.
19. https://youtube.com/shorts/HUUgYMHIPLo?feature=share.
20. Berland, J. (2019). *Virtual menageries: Animals as mediators in network cultures*. Cambridge, MA: The MIT Press, p. 2.
21. Berland, J. (2019). *Virtual menageries: Animals as mediators in network cultures*. Cambridge, MA: The MIT Press.
22. Berland, J. (2019). *Virtual menageries: Animals as mediators in network cultures*. Cambridge, MA: The MIT Press, p. 16.
23. Davies, S. (2012). *The artful species: Aesthetics, art, and evolution*. Oxford, UK: Oxford University Press, p. 80.
24. Davies, S. (2012). *The artful species: Aesthetics, art, and evolution*. Oxford, UK: Oxford University Press.
25. Kac, E. (2007). *Signs of life: Bio art and beyond*. Cambridge, MA: The MIT Press ; Groinowski, D. (1997). Aux commencements du rire moderne. L'esprit fumiste, José Corti, Paris.
26. https://www.bonhams.com/auctions/11928/lot/29/.
27. Cembalest, R. (2013). Birds do it, bees do it: Taking animals' art skills seriously. ArtNews. March 28. https://www.artnews.com/art-news/news/animals-making-art-2208/.
28. https://www.ucl.ac.uk/news/2012/jan/art-animals-comes-london.
29. Rohman, C. (2018). *Choreographies of the living*. Oxford, UK: Oxford University Press, p. 41.
30. Rohman, C. (2018). *Choreographies of the living*. Oxford, UK: Oxford University Press.
31. Busch, H., & Silver, B. (1994). *Why cats paint: A theory of feline aesthetics*. Berkeley, CA: Ten Speed Press.
32. Busch, H., & Silver, B. (1994). *Why cats paint: A theory of feline aesthetics*. Berkeley, CA: Ten Speed Press, p. 73.
33. Busch, H., & Silver, B. (1994). *Why cats paint: A theory of feline aesthetics*. Berkeley, CA: Ten Speed Press, p. 58.
34. Kac, E. (2007). *Signs of life: Bio art and beyond*. Cambridge, MA: The MIT Press.
35. Gessert, G. (2010). *Green light: Toward an art of evolution*. Cambridge, MA: The MIT Press.
36. http://marcquinn.com/artworks/single/dna-portrait-of-sir-john-sulston.
37. Harrower, J., Felice, G., Parker, J., Espinel, J.C., Harris, D., Hillary, F., & Ribeaux, T. (2022). The Algae Society BioArt Design Lab: Exploring multispecies

entanglements and making kin with algae. *Leonardo*, 55(4): 332–337. doi: https://doi.org/10.1162/leon_a_02184.

38. Aloi, J. (2022). Confluence. Esse. https://esse.ca/compte-rendu/confluence/.

39. http://algaesociety.org/blog/algae_digital_kaleidoscope_tapestry/.

40. openlabresearch.com.

41. Harrower, J., Parker, J., & Merson, M. (2018, July). Species loss: Exploring opportunities with art–science. *Integrative and Comparative Biology*, 58(1): 103–112, https://doi.org/10.1093/icb/icy016.

42. Voss-Andreae, J. (2013). Unraveling life's building blocks: Sculpture inspired by proteins. *Leonardo*, 46(1): 12–17. doi: https://doi.org/10.1162/LEON_a_00478.

43. https://isea-archives.siggraph.org/presentation/deciphering-realities-moving-frontiers-presented-by-trinidade-and-guillou/.

44. Gessert, G. (1993). Notes on genetic art. *Leonardo*, 26(3): 205–211. https://doi.org/10.2307/1575812.

45. https://www.clotmag.com/biomedia/joe-davis.

46. Lorusso, M. (2015). Microbioenergy theaters. *Leonardo*, 48(5): 430–433. doi: https://doi.org/10.1162/LEON_a_00923.

47. Savić, S., & Grant, S. (2022). Slime mold and network imaginaries: An experimental approach to communication. *Leonardo,* 55(5): 462–467. doi: https://doi.org/10.1162/leon_a_02248.

48. https://grist.org/article/this-artist-is-using-technology-to-bring-nature-back-into-the-city/.

49. Cembalest, R. (2013). Birds do it, bees do it: Taking animals' art skills seriously. ArtNews. March 28. https://www.artnews.com/art-news/news/animals-making-art-2208/.

50. https://youtu.be/FpUtsUnuDIQ.

51. https://fabricworkshopandmuseum.org/artist/maria-fernanda-cardoso/?doing_wp_cron=1664909618.3474979400634765625000.

52. http://www.conceptlab.com/roachbot/.

53. http://www.orlan.eu/.

54. https://digitalartarchive.at/database/general/work/poetica-vaginal.html.

55. https://www.symbiotica.uwa.edu.au/residents/zaretsky.

56. https://artscy.sites.ucsc.edu/2014/11/25/marion-laval-jeantet-and-benoit-mangin/.

57. Gessert, G. (2010). *Green light: Toward an art of evolution*. Cambridge, MA: The MIT Press ; Grau, O. (2003). *Virtual art: From illusion to immersion*. Cambridge, MA: The MIT Press ; Catts, O., & Zurr, I. (2002). Growing semi-living sculptures: The tissue culture art project. *Leonardo*, 35(4), 365–370 ; Catts, O., & Zurr, I. (2006). The tissue culture and art project: The semi-living as agents of irony. *Performance and technology: Practices of virtual embodiment and interactivity*, 153–168.

Conclusion

Beauty is not the sole domain of human beings. Rather than lessening the work of traditional artists, the transformative aesthetics described in this book expands our understanding of creativity. New technologies drive innovation in the arts. Instead of meeting the public desire for familiar types of artworks, artists utilizing an expanded conceptual framework can push boundaries.

The pandemic period of the early 2020s may be a turning point in artificial intelligence, when the effectiveness of neural networks to create documents and images made a leap in sophistication, combined with a change in the attitude of the public, as virtual work became the norm for many and there was time for self-reflection. Furthermore, the ongoing debate about computer consciousness centering on the notion of embodiment provokes the question of whether machines can be creative in ways paralleling humans. As computers grow in complexity, might machines start asking the reverse provocative question—can a human create art?[1]

The biological sciences at the beginning of the 21st century evolved as rapidly as computer science, with the unraveling of the genetic secrets of life, forcing questions about human uniqueness. The awe-inspiring images coming to us from NASA's James Webb Space Telescope emphasize the power of science to see other worlds, recentering the place of humans in the universe.

In this final chapter, strands of thinking about aesthetics, East and West, old and new, coalesce. The conceptions evolving out of centuries of diverse traditions are summarized, and the impact on individuals and larger social institutions are considered.

PRIMARY QUESTIONS

This book began with the following avenues of inquiry:

136   *Conclusion*

1. How might new computer and biological advancements affect our understanding of traditional aesthetics and artistic practice?
2. How does a knowledge of what has become known as everyday aesthetics (pervasive creativity) positively affect us?

Impact of Computer and Biological Advancements on Aesthetics

The traditional Western view of aesthetics presented in the first chapter displayed the themes of human-centeredness and finished imitative objects with delineated characteristics, art/science opposition, and an art/life disconnect. Transformative aesthetics, influenced by world cultures, instead focuses on ego-lessness, creative process, pervasive beauty, the blending of science and art, and seeking beauty in the actual world beyond boundaries.

As learned earlier, in the post–World War II era, American research centers such as Bell Laboratories and MIT intensified efforts to create a dynamic

Fig. c.1.   Galaxy Cluster SMACS 0723. NASA, ESA, CSA, and STScI

Table c.1. Traditional Versus New Aesthetics

Traditional Aesthetics	Transformative Aesthetics
Ego/Consciousness	Integration of Materiality and Spirituality
Finished Artwork	Process
Characteristics of Beauty	Pervasiveness of Beauty
Separation of Science and Art	Blending of Science and Art
Imitation	Ordinary

synergy between the arts and the rapidly evolving scientific world. This effort led directly to computer-based art forms, and an increased appreciation for beauty found, and sometimes manipulated, in the natural world.

The resistance to computer or digital art is, at its core, a form of anthropocentrism. Those who argue that computers can make art face a hostility like that experienced by scientists throughout history who moved humans conceptually from the center of the universe. At the very least, powerful new digital applications can mimic artistry and in so doing help us understand human creativity.

Some argue for a shift in thinking about computers from mere tools to collaborative partners. Many researchers advocate for a connection between machine creativity in a manner that is not in conflict with human artists and their emotional and social intentions. They urge a collaborative partnership between what humans or machines independently can creativity imagine.[2]

Kepes, writing in the catalogue for the 1970 *Explorations* Smithsonian exhibit, noted the important change coming from art integrated with new technologies:

> A centuries-old discarded framework for the artistic process, thus, has been revived in the newest evolutionary step in the development of the artistic community. In becoming a collaborative enterprise in which artists, scientists, urban planners, and engineers are interdependent, art clearly enters a new phase of orientation in which its prime goal is the revitalization of the entire human environment.[3]

For humans, working with machine intelligence can lead to an energized art form. While one can adjust algorithms, immediate control of the product is beyond the programmer. The mathematical formulas attempting to imitate genetic evolution or brain networks are outside specific control, and therefore the resulting artwork generated is strange and original in some sense. Those who examine digital artwork often find an otherworldly feel to it, which is difficult to pinpoint. One of the biggest barriers to popularity may be for humans to appreciate the eerie art pieces that are created through AI.[4]

Many scholars suggest the primary challenge with computer learning and art is one of consciousness. Can individual computers be aware of themselves like humans? Margaret Boden, in the *Creative Mind: Myths and Mechanisms*, elaborates on the difficulty wrestling with the computer consciousness question:

> If creativity necessarily involves conscious experience over and above the self-reflective evaluation of ideas, and if no computer could have conscious experience, then no computer could "really" be creative. But these are very iffy ifs. The question must remain open—not just because we do not know the answer, but because we do not clearly understand how to ask the question.[5]

Michael Graziano, a neuroscientist at Princeton University, believes that computers will develop consciousness. In the same way that human consciousness evolved, he argues that such a mental state can be developed in computers as well. Graziano sees mind becoming decoupled from biology and the line between artificial intelligence and human intelligence blurring beyond recognition. According to him, we are close to understanding consciousness well enough to build it and transform our civilization in doing so. In this way, the final hold of human beings on art may dissolve.[6]

On the biological front, Marian Dawkins, in her book *Through Our Eyes Only? The Search for Animal Consciousness*, argues that "consciousness" is a mysterious concept, and that the question of non-human self-awareness, if answered, is important because it may bring other living organisms inside the human sphere.[7] In biological art, many of the central questions asked in this book from the start are pushed to the limit. Overall, Dawkins argues, there are more similarities between humans and animals than supposed. "We have seen case after case where animal behavior has turned out to be sophisticated and often more complex and baffling than even the people who were studying it had anticipated."[8]

Biological and computer art strongly impact a discussion of aesthetics. By extending creative properties to nature and machines, we uncover a more profound understanding of the world humans inhabit.

Power of Everyday Aesthetics

Everyday aesthetics incorporates recurring world culture beliefs and encourages ego-less art making, creative process over finished product, an appreciation of pervasive beauty, and the integration of technologies (mechanical and biological) and art. The emergent philosophy is just beginning to grasp the influence these principles might have on individuals, artists, and communities.

Marcia Mueller Eaton, in *Aesthetics and the Good Life*, contends that having aesthetic experiences is one of life's central goals, and that such activities and responses enrich life. The aesthetic is marked by attending to and reflecting upon a thing's intrinsic properties and by the delight that accompanies this attention and reflection. "An experience is aesthetic if there is delight taken in an intrinsic feature of an object or event, and that feature is traditionally considered worth attending to, that is, worth perceiving or reflecting upon."[9]

Alva Noë, in *Strange Tools: Art and Human Nature*, maintains that our lives are structured by organization, and that artistic practice brings our organization into view, and in doing this, art reorganizes us. Art removes tools from their settings and makes them strange or unfamiliar, bringing out what been taken for granted. We make tools strange to investigate ourselves.

> They organize our lives and, in part, make us what we are. Works of art put our making practices and our tendency to rely on what we make, and so also our practices of thinking and talking and making pictures, on display. Art puts us on display. Art unveils us to ourselves.[10]

John Kaag, in his book entitled *Hiking with Nietzsche: On Becoming Who You Are*, claims that Nietzsche found a way to make the suffering and sudden endings of life beautiful and aesthetically significant. This is what Nietzsche meant in *The Birth of Tragedy* when he claimed that existence can be justified only as an aesthetic experience. The ancient Greeks understood beauty as a way of transforming agony and drudgery into something creative and enrapturing. The point is to view the tensions and contradictions of life as one would take in a work of art.

Some contemporary views of aesthetics focus on interpersonal and psychological aspects of beauty. Piero Ferriccui, in his book, *Beauty and the Soul: The Extraordinary Power of Everyday Beauty to Heal Your Life*, asks how life changes for individuals open to beauty. According to him, "Beauty is not like a distant satellite, but like a sun that gives life and light to all areas of our life."[11] Furthermore, creating and appreciating beauty is often a social experience leading to a greater capacity to understand others, adapt to their way of thinking, and live in an increasingly multicultural world. Finally, a concentration on beauty fights excessive materialism: "If we can see beauty at every street corner, we will be far less concerned with ownership, because we will know that beauty is a nonmaterial and renewable good, ever ready to appear and surprise us in daily life."[12]

How can we find more beauty in our lives? Through numerous interviews, Ferriccui discovered commonalities regarding how people engage beauty. It is important to be vulnerable and hold no preconceived idea about what is beautiful. Beauty is often discovered in solitude but born with sharing. According to Ferriccui, when we appreciate beauty, we are open, defenseless, and not playing expected roles. One way to find more beauty in life is to simply lengthen time by listening closely and looking for longer. When we are forced to discover again the art of being slow, we discover the rhythm of realization and enjoyment.

Finally, the power in everyday aesthetics is likely be seen in evolving institutions of culture, especially museums. Dewey contends that the museum conception of art fails to recognize the works of art in everyday experience and is essentially anti-democratic.

> Most European museums are, among other things, memorials of the rise of nationalism and imperialism. Every capital must have its own museum of painting, sculpture, etc.; devoted in part to exhibiting the greatness of its artistic past, and, in other part, to exhibiting the loot gathered by its monarchs in conquest of other nations; for instance, the accumulations of the spoils of Napoleon that are in the Louvre.[13]

In opposition to museum art, Dewey describes how authentic art functions by invigorating the meaning of ordinary objects and creating a new experience. Sometimes the expansion and intensification are brought about by means of simple appreciation of daily life, or by recontextualizing. At root this type of art pursues full and intense experiences of the common world in its fullness. "It does so by reducing the raw-materials of that experience to matter ordered through form."[14]

Indian philosophy claims that if we could return to a sense of the artistry and dignity of labor, to the usefulness of beauty, and to the immanence of the spiritual in the physical world, we can restore ourselves to reality.

> A natural effect of the Museum exhibition will be to lead the public to enquire why it is that objects of "museum quality" are to be found only in Museums and are not in daily use and readily obtainable. For the Museum objects, on the whole, were not originally "treasures" made to be seen in glass cases, but rather common objects of the marketplace that could have been bought and used by anyone.[15]

Furthermore, the idea that productions of fine art are useless mocks a free society:

> We have gone so far as to divorce work from culture, and to think of culture as something to be acquired in hours of leisure; but there can be only a hothouse and unreal culture where work itself is not its means; if culture does not show itself in all we make we are not cultured.[16]

Arthur Danto contends that as art evolves, so must museums, making the provocative tie of museums to the guillotine:

I have heard it said that the museum and the guillotine were invented together, and in historical truth they do refer to one another, for it was in part works confiscated from those whose heads were severed in the revolutionary fervor that formed the contents of the first museum in the modern sense of the term.[17]

He points out that possession of art was a symbol of authority, a symbolic appropriation of authority. In the French Revolution, power was symbolically transferred to the people from their rulers when their art was seized. He argues that museums have become too important in contemporary culture to be only storehouses of symbolic authority.[18]

Those places we typically think of as the defenders of high art and culture are pressured by new aesthetics to change. Dewey urged the democratization of art. Leaders in digital art, such as Google's Agüera y Arcas, see the rapid revolution from AI as a similar promise to democratize the means of the production of art.[19]

CONCLUSION

Edward Bullough, the first to lecture on aesthetics at Cambridge University, captured the significance of art experiences in life:

> What we are, the sum total of our most personal being, we undoubtedly owe in a much larger degree to experiences made through the medium of aesthetic impressions, than to the extension of our personality by contact with the real world. If we could subtract all the wealth bestowed upon us by Art, it is inconceivable how little would be left of what we now feel ourselves to possess.[20]

A world without art isn't possible if we find beauty everywhere.

Now at the end of this enterprise to better understand art in a 21st-century context of remarkable technological change, it appears to the author that the new developments arose from centuries of human history, a back-and-forth in asserting human uniqueness, reaching for ecstatic experiences, and being awed by revelations of beauty found surrounding us in the natural world. Yes, it is frightening to look without self, share creativity with nature and other living organisms, and appreciate the overwhelming power of technology. Yet far from diminishing, grasping the beauty of the everyday world on the ground before us and up in the astounding galaxies beyond us, engenders significance.

NOTES

1. A.A. Berg, personal communication, April 3, 2023.
2. Mazzone, M., & Elgammal, A. (2019). Art, creativity, and the potential of artificial intelligence. *Arts*, 8(1): 26. MDPI AG. Retrieved from http://dx.doi.org/10.3390/arts8010026 ; McCormack, J., & d'Inverno, M. (2014). On the future of computers and creativity. In AISB 2014 Symposium on Computational Creativity, London.
3. Smithsonian Institution Archives. Record Unit 333, Box 9, Folder: Explorations, p. 38.
4. Audry, S. (2021). *Art in the age of machine learning*. Cambridge, MA: MIT Press.
5. Boden, M.A. (2004). *The creative mind: Myths and mechanisms*. London, UK: Routledge, pp. 296–297.
6. Graziano, M.S.A. (2019). *Rethinking consciousness: A scientific theory of subjective experience*. New York: W.W. Norton & Company.
7. Dawkins, M.S. (1993). *Through our eyes only? The search for animal consciousness*. Oxford, UK: W.H. Freeman.
8. Dawkins, M.S. (1993). *Through our eyes only? The search for animal consciousness*. Oxford, UK: W.H. Freeman, p. 62.
9. Eaton, M.M. (1989). *Aesthetics and the good life*. Cranbury, NJ: Associated University Presses, p. 147.
10. Noë, A. (2015). *Strange tools: Art and human nature*. New York: Hill and Wang, p. 101.
11. Ferriccui, P. (2010). *Beauty and the soul: The extraordinary power of everyday beauty to heal your life*. New York: TarcherPerigee, p. 2.
12. Ferriccui, P. (2010). *Beauty and the soul: The extraordinary power of everyday beauty to heal your life*. New York: TarcherPerigee, p. 23.
13. Dewey, J. (1934b). *Art as experience*. New York: The Berkley Publishing Group, p. 7.
14. Dewey, J. (1934b). *Art as experience*. New York: The Berkley Publishing Group, p. 138.
15. Coomaraswamy, A.K. (1956). *Christian and oriental philosophy of art*. New York: Dover Publications Inc., p. 13.
16. Coomaraswamy, A.K. (1956). *Christian and oriental philosophy of art*. New York: Dover Publications Inc., p. 15.
17. Danto, A.C. (1986). *Encounters & reflections: Art in the historical present*. New York: HarperCollins, p. 317.
18. Danto, A.C. (1986). *Encounters & reflections: Art in the historical present*. New York: HarperCollins.
19. Blaise Agüera, y. A. (2017). Art in the age of machine intelligence†. *Arts*, 6(4): 18. doi:https://doi.org/10.3390/arts6040018.
20. Bullough, E. (1957). *Aesthetics: Lectures and essays*. London, UK: Bowes & Bowes, p. 88.

Bibliography

Aiken, N.E. (1998). *The biological origins of art*. Westport, CT: Praeger.
Alexander, S. R. (2021). "Oh my god!" exploring ecstatic experience through the evocative technology of gospel choir (Order No. 28772774). Available from ProQuest Central; Publicly Available Content Database. (2597477886). Retrieved from http://ezproxy.lapl.org/login?url=https://www.proquest.com/dissertations-theses/oh-my-god-exploring-ecstatic-experience-through/docview/2597477886/se-2.
Alland, A. (1977). *The artistic animal: An inquiry into the biological roots of art*. Garden City, NY: Anchor Books.
Alpaydin, E. (2020). *Introduction to machine learning*. Cambridge, MA: The MIT Press.
Appleton, H., & Nelstrop, L. (eds). (2018). *Art and mysticism: Interfaces in the medieval and modern periods*. New York: Routledge.
Aristotle. (1941). *The basic works of Aristotle*. New York: Random House.
Armstrong, J. (2005). *The secret power of beauty: Why happiness is in the eye of the beholder*. London, UK: Penguin Books.
Ashley, K. (2022). *The art of prompts for artificial intelligence: Make art with DALL-E, Midjourney and Livebook AI (Awesome AI)*. Independently Published.
Audry, S. (2021). *Art in the age of machine learning*. Cambridge, MA: MIT Press.
Audry, S., & Ippolito, J. (2019). Can artificial intelligence make art without artists? ask the viewer. *Arts*, 8(1). doi:https://doi.org/10.3390/arts8010035.
Begbie, J. (2018). *Redeeming transcendence in the arts: Bearing witness to the triune god*. Grand Rapids, MI: Eerdmans Publishing Co.
Berland, J. (2019). *Virtual menageries: Animals as mediators in network cultures*. Cambridge, MA: The MIT Press.
Berleant. A. (1991). *Art and engagement*. Philadelphia, PA: Temple University Press.
Berg, G.A. (2022). *A career in the arts: The complex learning and career needs of creative professionals*. New York: Rowman & Littlefield.
Bhattacharyya, A. (2020). From a context-bound to an essentializing conception: A study of Longinus's treatise on the sublime. *Journal of Comparative Literature and Aesthetics*, 43(2), 102–11. Retrieved from http://ezproxy.lapl.org/login?url=https:

//www.proquest.com/scholarly-journals/context-bound-essentializing-conception-study/docview/2465482262/se-2?accountid=6749.

Blaise Agüera, y. A. (2017). Art in the age of machine intelligence†. *Arts*, 6(4), 18. doi:https://doi.org/10.3390/arts6040018.

Blakinger, J.R. (2019). *Undreaming the Bauhaus*. Cambridge, MA: The MIT Press.

Boden, M.A. (2004). *The creative mind: Myths and mechanisms*. London, UK: Routledge.

Boivin, N. (2008). *Material cultures, material minds: The impact of things on human thought, society, and evolution*. Cambridge, UK: Cambridge University Press.

Bonabeau, E., Dorigo, M., & Theraulaz, G. (1999) *Swarm intelligence*. Oxford, UK: Oxford University Press.

Bowker, J. (2000). Mysticism. In *The Concise Oxford Dictionary of World Religions*. Oxford University Press. Retrieved 30 Dec. 2021, from https://www-oxfordreference-com.ezproxy.lapl.org/view/10.1093/acref/9780192800947.001.0001/acref-9780192800947-e-5021.

Brand, H., & Chaplin, A. (2001). *Art & soul: Signposts for Christians in the arts*. Carlisle, UK: Piquant.

Brett. (2020). Libby Heaney bridges the gap between Science and Art. A former Quantum Scientist she is now a full-time artist. Quantum Zeitgeist, October 19. https://quantumzeitgeist.com/libby-heaney-bridges-the-gap-between-science-and-art-a-former-quantum-scientist-she-is-now-a-full-time-artist/.

Brodsky, J.K. (2002). *Dismantling the patriarchy, bit by bit: Art, feminism, and digital technology*. London, UK: Bloomsbury Visual Arts.

Bronowski, J. (1965). The discovery of form. In Kepes, G. (ed.), *Structure in art and in science*. New York: George Braziller.

Brooks, R.A. (2002) *Flesh and machines: how robots will change us*. New York: Pantheon Books.

Bullough, E. (1957). *Aesthetics: Lectures and essays*. London, UK: Bowes & Bowes.

Busch, H., & Silver, B. (1994). *Why cats paint: A theory of feline aesthetics*. Berkeley, CA: Ten Speed Press.

Bychkov. V. (2021). The Russian Symbolist Viacheslav Ivanov on Aesthetic Experience as Religious. *Religions*, 12 (2), 68. http://dx.doi.org/10.3390/rel12020068.

Carlson, A. (2009). *Nature & Landscape: An introduction to environmental aesthetics*. New York: Columbia University Press.

Carpenter, E. (1966). Image making in artic art. In Kepes, G. (ed), *Sign image symbol*. New York: George Braziller.

Catts, O., & Zurr, I. (2002). Growing semi-living sculptures: The tissue culture art project. *Leonardo*, 35(4): 365–370. doi: https://doi.org/10.1162/002409402760181123.

Catts, O., & Zurr, I. (2006). The tissue culture and art project: The semi-living as agents of irony. *Performance and technology: Practices of virtual embodiment and interactivity*, 153–168.

Cembalest, R. (2013). Birds do it, bees do it: Taking animals' art skills seriously. ArtNews. March 28. https://www.artnews.com/art-news/news/animals-making-art-2208/.

Chalmers, D.J. (2010). *The character of consciousness*. Oxford, UK: Oxford University Press.
Chaudhary, A. (1991). *Comparative aesthetics: East and West*. Delhi, India: Eastern Book Linkers.
Clarke, M., Dufeu, F., & Manning, P. (2020). *Inside computer music*. Oxford, UK: Oxford University Press.
Coleman, E.J. (1998). *Creativity and spirituality: Bonds between art and religion*. Albany, NY: State University of New York Press.
Collingwood, R.G. (1938). *The principles of art*. Oxford, UK: Oxford at the Clarendon Press.
Coomaraswamy, A.K. (1956). *Christian and oriental philosophy of art*. New York: Dover Publications, Inc.
Csikszentmihalyi, M. (1996). *Creativity: Flow and the psychology of discovery and invention*. New York: HarperCollins.
Danto, A.C. (1986). *Encounters & reflections: Art in the historical present*. New York: HarperCollins.
Danto, A. (1987). The art world. In Margolis, J. (ed.), *Philosophy looks at the arts: Contemporary readings in aesthetics*. Philadelphia, PA: Temple University Press.
Davies, S. (2012). *The artful species: Aesthetics, art, and evolution*. Oxford, UK: Oxford University Press.
Dawkins, M.S. (1993). *Through our eyes only? The search for animal consciousness*. Oxford: UK: W.H. Freeman.
Dehaene, S. (2014). *Consciousness and the brain: Deciphering how the brain codes our thoughts*. New York: Penguin.
Dewey, J. (1934). *A common faith*. New Haven, CT: Yale University Press.
Dewey, J. (1934b). *Art as experience*. New York: The Berkley Publishing Group.
Díaz-Gilbert, M. (2018). The ascetic life of the ultrarunner. *Spiritus*, 18(2), 201–217. doi:http://dx.doi.org/10.1353/scs.2018.0025.
Dissanayake, E. (2000). *Art and intimacy: How the arts began*. Seattle, WA: University of Washington Press.
Dixon, S. (2007). *Digital performance: A history of new media in theater, dance, performance art, and installation*. Cambridge, MA: The MIT Press.
Dreyfus, H.L. (1972). *What computers can't do: A critique of artificial reason*. New York: Harper & Row.
Dyrness, W.A. (2001). *Visual faith: Art, theology, and worship in dialogue*. Grand Rapids, MI: Baker Academic.
Eaton, M.M. (1989). *Aesthetics and the good life*. Cranbury, NJ: Associated University Presses.
Eco, U. (2002). *Art and beauty in the middle ages*. New Haven, CT: Yale University Press.
Ehrenzweig, A. (1967). *The hidden order of art: A study in the psychology of artistic imagination*. Berkeley, CA: University of California Press.

Elgammal, A., Liu, B., Elhoseiny, M., & Mazzone, M. (2017). Can: Creative adversarial networks, generating "art" by learning about styles and deviating from style norms. arXiv preprint arXiv:1706.07068.

Eliade, M. (1990). *Symbolism, the sacred, and the arts.* New York: The Crossroad Publishing Company.

Elkins, J., & Morgan, D. (2009) *Re-enchantment.* New York: Routledge.

Ferriccui, P. (2010). *Beauty and the soul: The extraordinary power of everyday beauty to heal your life.* New York: TarcherPerigee.

Fingesten, P. (1961) Spirituality, mysticism and non-Objective art. *Art Journal*, 21(1): 2–6. DOI: 10.1080/00043249.1961.10794175.

Forsey, J. (2016). *The aesthetics of design.* Oxford, UK: Oxford University Press.

Frank, P. (2020). *Sharing code: Art1, Frederick Hammersley, and the dawn of computer art.* Santa Fe: NM: Museum of New Mexico Press.

Fuller, B. (1965). Conceptuality of fundamental structures. In Kepes, G. (ed.), *Structure in art and in science.* New York: George Braziller.

Fujimura, M. (2020). *Art and faith: A theology of making.* New Haven, CT: Yale University Press.

Gablik, S. (1998). *The enchantment of art.* London, UK: Thames and Hudson.

Gessert, G. (1993). Notes on genetic art. *Leonardo*, 26(3), 205–211. https://doi.org/10.2307/1575812.

Gessert, G. (2010). *Green light: Toward an art of evolution.* Cambridge, MA: The MIT Press.

Gleiser, M. (2022). *Great minds don't think alike: Debates on Consciousness, reality, intelligence, faith, time, AI, immortality, and the human.* New York: Columbia University Press.

Glowacki, D., Tew, P., Hyde, J., Kriefman, L., Mitchell, T., Price, J., & McIntosh-Smith, S. (2013). Using human energy fields to sculpt real-time molecular dynamics. In L. Fruk, & P. Weibel (Eds.), *Molecular aesthetics.* Cambridge, MA: MIT Press.

Gombrich, E.H. (1996). *The essential Gombrich.* London, UK: Phaidon.

Goodfellow, I., Pouget-Abadie, J., Mirza, M., Xu, B., Warde-Farley, D., Ozair, S., ... & Bengio, Y. (2020). Generative adversarial networks. *Communications of the ACM*, 63(11): 139–144.

Grau, O. (2003). *Virtual art: From illusion to immersion.* Cambridge, MA: The MIT Press.

Graziano, M.S.A. (2019). *Rethinking consciousness: A scientific theory of subjective experience.* New York: W.W. Norton & Company.

Greenfield, G. (2014). Penousal Machado; swarm art. *Leonardo*, 47(1): 5–7. doi: https://doi.org/10.1162/LEON_a_00695.

Gristwood, S., & Kawano, H. (2019). Japan's pioneer of computer arts. *Leonardo*, 52(1): 75–80. doi: https://doi.org/10.1162/leon_a_01605.

Gropius, W. (1956). Reorientation. In Kepes, G. (ed.), *The new landscape in art and science.* Chicago, IL: Paul Theobald and Co.

Haapala, A., Levinson, J., & Rantala, V. (1997). *The end of art and beyond: Essays after Danto.* Atlantic Highlands, NJ: Humanities Press International.

Hadjeres, G., Pachet, F., & Nielson, F. (2017). DeepBach: A Steerable Model for Bach Chorales Generation. Proceedings of the 34th International Conference on Machine Learning, PMLR 70:1362–1371.

Harrower, J., Felice, G., Parker, J., Espinel, J.C., Harris, D., Hillary, F., & Ribeaux, T. (2022). The algae society bioart design lab: Exploring multispecies entanglements and making kin with algae. *Leonardo*, 55(4): 332–337. doi: https://doi.org/10.1162/leon_a_02184.

Harrower, J., Parker, J., & Merson, M. (2018). Species loss: Exploring opportunities with art–science. *Integrative and Comparative Biology*, 58(1): 103–112. https://doi.org/10.1093/icb/icy016.

Herwitz, D. (2008). *Aesthetics: Key concepts in philosophy*. London, UK: Continuum International Publishing Group.

Hodgkinson, V.A., & Weitzman, M.S. (1993). *From belief to commitment: The community service activities and finances of religious congregations in the United States*. Washington DC: Independent Sector.

Irvin, S. (2019). The pervasiveness of the aesthetic in ordinary experience. In Lamarque, P., & Olsen, S.H. (eds.) *Aesthetics and the philosophy of art: The analytic tradition*. Hoboken, NJ: Wiley Blackwell.

Jessop, E. (2015). Capturing the body live: A framework for technological recognition and extension of physical expression in performance. *Leonardo*, 48(1): 32–38. doi: https://doi.org/10.1162/LEON_a_00935.

Johnston, A. (2015). Conversational interaction in interactive dance works. Leonardo, 48(3): 296–297. 296–97. doi: https://doi.org/10.1162/LEON_a_01017.

Johnson, R.A. (1989). *Ecstasy: Understanding the psychology of joy*. San Francisco, CA: HarperCollins.

Johnstone, S. (ed). (2008). *The everyday: Documents of contemporary art*. Boston, MA: MIT Press.

Johung, J. (2015). Choreographic arrhythmias. *Leonardo*, 48(2): 172–173. doi: https://doi.org/10.1162/LEON_a_00975.

Juniper, A. (2003). *Wabi Sabi: The Japanese art of impermanence*. Tokyo, Japan: Tuttle Publishing.

Kaag, J. (2020). *Sick souls, healthy minds: How William James can save your life*. Princeton, NJ: Princeton University Press.

Kac, E. (2007). *Signs of life: Bio art and beyond*. Cambridge, MA: The MIT Press.

Kepes, G. (ed.) (1956). *The new landscape in art and science*. Chicago, IL: Paul Theobald and Co.

Khan, H. I. (1996). *The mysticism of sound and music: The Sufi teaching of Hazrat Inayat Khan*. Boston, MA: Shambhala Dragon Editions.

Kupfer, J.H. (1983). *Experience as art: Aesthetics in everyday life*. Albany, NY: State University of New York Press.

Kuspit, D. (2004). *The end of art*. Cambridge, UK: Cambridge University Press.

Leach, J., & deLahunta, S. (2017). Dance becoming knowledge: Designing a digital "body." *Leonardo*, 50(5): 461–467. doi: https://doi.org/10.1162/LEON_a_01074.

Lipsey, R. (1988). *An art of our own: The spiritual in twentieth century art*. Berkeley, CA: Shambhala Publications.

Lorusso, M. (2015). Microbioenergy theaters. *Leonardo*, 48(5): 430–433. doi: https://doi.org/10.1162/LEON_a_00923.
Manning, R.R. (2009). *The Cambridge companion to Paul Tillich*. Cambridge, UK: Cambridge University Press.
Maquet, J. (1986). *The aesthetic experience: An anthropologist looks at the visual arts*. New Haven, CT: Yale University Press.
Maritain, J. (1953). *Creative intuition in art and poetry*. New York: Pantheon Books.
Martin, J. (2002). *The education of John Dewey: A biography*. New York: Columbia University Press.
Marra, M.F. (2001). *A history of modern Japanese aesthetics*. Oahu, HI: University of Hawaii Press.
Martindale, C. (1990). *The clockwork muse: The predictability of artistic change*. New York: Basic Books.
Martland, T.R. (1981). *Religion and art: An interpretation*. Albany, NY: New York State University Press.
Mattes, M.C. (2017). *Martin Luther's theology of beauty: A reappraisal*. Grand Rapids, MI: Baker Academics.
Mazzone, M., & Elgammal, A. (2019). Art, creativity, and the potential of artificial intelligence. *Arts*, 8(1), 26. MDPI AG. Retrieved from http://dx.doi.org/10.3390/arts8010026.
McCarren, F. (2003). *Dancing machines: Choreographies of the age of mechanical reproduction*. Stanford, CA: Sanford University Press.
McCormack, J., & d'Inverno, M. (2014). On the future of computers and creativity. In AISB 2014 Symposium on Computational Creativity, London.
McCormick, J., Hossny, M., Fielding, M., Mullins, J., Vincent, J.B., Hossny, M., Vincs, K., Mohamed, S., Nahavandi, S., Creighton, D., & Hutchison, S. (2020). Feels like dancing: Motion capture-driven haptic interface as an added sensory experience for dance viewing. *Leonardo*, 53(1): 45–49. doi: https://doi.org/10.1162/leon_a_01689.
McDonald, M., & Walton, J.M. (2007). *The Cambridge companion to Greek and Roman theatre*. Cambridge, UK: Cambridge University Press.
Metzinger, T. (2010). *The ego tunnel: The science of the mind and the myth of the self*. New York: Basic Books.
Michie, D. (1968). Computer—servant or master. *Spectrum*. No. 45.
Miller, A.I. (2019). *The artist in the machine: The world of AI-powered creativity*. Cambridge, MA: MIT Press.
Miller, K.A. (1997). *Wisdom comes dancing: Selected writings of Ruth St. Denis on dance, spirituality, and the body*. Seattle, WA: Peace Works.
Mitchell, T., Hyde, J., Tew, P., & Glowacki, D.R. (2016). Danceroom spectroscopy: At the frontiers of physics, performance, interactive art and technology. *Leonardo*, 49(2): 138–147. doi: https://doi.org/10.1162/LEON_a_00924.
Mithen, S. (2006). *The singing Neanderthals*. Cambridge, MA: Harvard University Press.
Morris, C. (1956). Man-cosmos symbols. In Kepes, G. (ed.), *The new landscape in art and science*. Chicago, IL: Paul Theobald and Co.

Moura, L. (2018). Robot art: An interview with Leonel Moura. *Arts*, 7(3): 28–. https://doi.org/10.3390/arts7030028.
Mukherji, R. (1991). *Comparative aesthetics: Indian and Western*. Calcutta, India: Sanskrit Pustak Bhandar.
Murdoch, I. (1999). *Existentialists and mystics: Writings on philosophy and literature*. New York: Penguin Books.
Nakayasu, A. (2020). Animated robotic sculptures: Using SMA motion display to create lifelike movements. *Leonardo*, 53(4): 419–423. doi: https://doi.org/10.1162/leon_a_01929.
Nasr, S. H. (1987). *Islamic art and spirituality*. Albany, NY: State University of New York Press.
Nettl, B. (2015). *The study of ethnomusicology: Thirty-three discussions*. Urbana, IL: University of Illinois Press.
Newton, S.J. (2001). *Painting, psychoanalysis, and spirituality*. Cambridge, UK: Cambridge University Press.
Nietzsche, F. (1927). *The philosophy of Nietzsche*. New York: The Modern Library.
Noë, A. (2015). *Strange tools: Art and human nature*. New York: Hill and Wang.
Noll, A. M. (1967). The digital computer as a creative medium. IEEE Spectrum. Vol. 4, no. 10, October.
Noy, S., & Zhang, W. (2023). Experimental evidence on the productivity effects of generative artificial intelligence. Unpublished MIT paper. https://economics.mit.edu/sites/default/files/inline-files/Noy_Zhang_1.pdf.
Odin, S. (2001). *Artistic detachment in Japan and the West: Psychic distance in comparative aesthetics*. Honolulu, HI: University of Hawaii Press.
Osmond, S. F. (1998, April). Art and the resurgent spiritual. *World and I*, 13(4): 100+. https://link.gale.com/apps/doc/A21185191/PPFA?u=lapl&sid=bookmark-PPFA&xid=9144c074.
Patterson, Z. (2015). *Peripheral vision: Bell labs, the S-C 4020, and the origins of computer art*. Cambridge, MA: The MIT Press.
Pattison, G. (1991). *Art, modernity and faith: Towards a theology of art*. New York: St. Martin's Press.
Plato. (1941). *The republic of Plato*. Oxford, UK: Oxford University Press.
Pollitt, J.J. (1972). *Art and experience in classical Greece*. Cambridge, UK: Cambridge University Press.
Rao, G.H. (1974). *Comparative aesthetics: Eastern and Western*. India: Mysore Printing and Publishing House.
Rohman, C. (2018). *Choreographies of the living*. Oxford, UK: Oxford University Press.
Saito, Y. (2017). *Aesthetics of the familiar: Everyday life and world-making*. Oxford, UK: Oxford University Press.
Saito, Y. (2021). Aesthetics of the everyday. In Zalta, E. N. (ed.), *The Stanford encyclopedia of philosophy*. https://plato.stanford.edu/archives/spr2021/entries/aesthetics-of-everyday/.
Saliers, D.E. (2007). *Music and theology*. Nashville, TN: Abingdon Press.

Sartwell, C. (1995). *The art of living: Aesthetics of the ordinary in world spiritual traditions*. Albany, NY: State University of New York Press.
Sartwell, C. (2003). Aesthetics of the everyday. In Levinson, J. *The Oxford handbook of aesthetics*. Oxford, UK: Oxford University Press.
Savić, S., & Grant, S. (2022). Slime mold and network imaginaries: An experimental approach to communication. *Leonardo*, 55(5): 462–467. doi: https://doi.org/10.1162/leon_a_02248.
Scharfstein, B. (1988). *Of birds, beasts, and other artists: An essay on the universality of art*. New York: New York University Press.
Shusterman, R. (2010). Dewey's art as experience: The psychological background. *Journal of Aesthetic Education*, 44(1): 26–43.
Smith, C.S. (1965). Structure substructure superstructure. In Kepes, G. (ed.), *Structure in art and in science*. New York: George Braziller.
Simon, H.A. (2019). *The sciences of the artificial*. Cambridge, MA: The MIT Press.
Skrbina, D. (2005). *Panpsychism in the West*. Cambridge, MA: The MIT Press.
Smith, P.H. (2004). *The body of the artisan: Art and experience in the scientific revolution*. Chicago, IL: The University of Chicago Press.
Spirituality and Christian Art. (2013). In Jones, T. D., Murray, L., & Murray, P. (Eds.), *The Oxford dictionary of Christian art and architecture*. Oxford, UK: Oxford University Press. Retrieved 30 Dec. 2021, from https://www-oxfordreference-com.ezproxy.lapl.org/view/10.1093/acref/9780199680276.001.0001/acref-9780199680276-e-1677.
Sprigge, T.L.S. (1974). *Santayana: An examination of his philosophy*. London, UK: Routledge.
Steele, J. (2002). *Architecture and computers*. New York: Watson-Guptill Publications.
Swann, P. C. (1958). *A concise history of Japanese art*. Tokyo, Japan: Kodansha International Ltd.
Sullivan, M. (1967). *A short history of Chinese art*. Berkeley, CA: University of California Press.
Suzuki, D.T. (1973). *Zen and Japanese culture*. Princeton, NJ: Princeton University Press.
Swann, P. C. (1958). *A concise history of Japanese art*. Tokyo, Japan: Kodansha International Ltd.
Taylor, G.D. (2014). *When the machine made art: The troubled history of computer art*. London, UK: Bloomsbury.
Thompson, R. (2014). Tirtha Prasad Mukhopadhyay; aesthetics of biocybernetic designs: A systems approach to biorobots and its implications for the environment. *Leonardo*, 47(4): 318–324. doi: https://doi.org/10.1162/LEON_a_00836.
Turing, A.M. (1950). Computing machinery and intelligence. *Mind*, LIX(236): 433–460. https://doi.org/10.1093/mind/LIX.236.433.
Unander-Scharin, A., & Unander-Scharin, C. (2016). Robocygne: Dancing life into an animal-human-machine. *Leonardo*, 49(3): 212–219. doi: https://doi.org/10.1162/LEON_a_01021.
Van Ness, P.H. (1996). *Spirituality and the secular quest*. New York: The Crossroad Publishing Company.

Venbrux, E., Rosi, P.S., & Welsch, R.L. (2006). *Exploring world art*. Long Grove, IL: Waveland Press, Inc.

Visona, M.B., Poynor, R., Cole, H.M., & Harris, M.D. (2001). *A history of art in Africa*. London, UK: Harry N. Abrams, Inc., Publishers.

Voss-Andreae, J. (2013). Unraveling life's building blocks: Sculpture inspired by proteins. *Leonardo*, 46(1): 12–17. doi: https://doi.org/10.1162/LEON_a_00478.

Weibel, P., & Fruk, L. (eds). (2014). *Molecular aesthetics*. Cambridge, MA: The MIT Press.

Witherspoon, G. (1977). *Language and art in the Navajo universe*. Ann Arbor, MI: University of Michigan Press.

Wilkinson, E.M., & Willoughby, L.A. (eds.) (1982) *Friedrich Schiller on the aesthetic education of man: In a series of letters*. Oxford, UK: Oxford University Press.

Willett, F. (2002). *African art*. London. New York: Thames & Hudson.

Wulf, A. (2022). *Magnificent rebels: The first Romantics and the invention of the self*. New York: Alfred A. Knopf.

Wuthnow, R. (2001). *Creative spirituality: The way of the artist*. Berkeley, CA: University of California Press.

Yanagi, S. (2019). *The beauty of everyday things*. New York: Penguin Modern Classics.

Yoshimatsu, J. (2011). The art in the everyday: A spiritual journey of aesthetic experience within western and Japanese contexts (Order No. 3484380). Available from ProQuest Central; Publicly Available Content Database. (903257084). Retrieved from http://ezproxy.lapl.org/login?url=https://www.proquest.com/dissertations-theses/art-everyday-spiritual-journey-aesthetic/docview/903257084/se-2.

Zhang, K., Harrell, S., & Ji, X. (2012). Computational aesthetics: On the complexity of computer-generated paintings. *Leonardo*, 45(3): 243–248. doi: https://doi.org/10.1162/LEON_a_00366.

Zhang, K., & Yu, J. (2016). Generation of Kandinsky art. *Leonardo*, 49(1): 48–54. doi: https://doi.org/10.1162/LEON_a_00908.

Zijlmans, K., & Van Damme, W. (2008). *World art studies: Exploring concepts and approaches*. Amsterdam: Valiz.

www.ingramcontent.com/pod-product-compliance
Lightning Source LLC
Chambersburg PA
CBHW020741230426
43665CB00009B/516